CHANGING THE MIND OF MISSIONS

WHERE HAVE WE GONE WRONG?

James F. Engel & William A. Dyrness

InterVarsity Press
Downers Grove, Illinois

InterVarsity Press
P.O. Box 1400, Downers Grove, IL 60515
World Wide Web: www.ivpress.com
E-mail: mail@ivpress.com

InterVarsity Press® is the book-publishing division of InterVarsity Christian Fellowship/USA®, a student
movement active on campus at hundreds of universities, colleges and schools of nursing in the United
States of America, and a member movement of the International Fellowship of Evangelical Students. For
information about local and regional activities, write Public Relations Dept., InterVarsity Christian
Fellowship/USA, 6400 Schroeder Rd., P.O. Box 7895, Madison, WI 53707-7895.

All Scripture quotations, unless otherwise indicated, are taken from the Holy Bible, New International
Version®. NIV®. Copyright ©1973, 1978, 1984 by International Bible Society. Used by permission of
Zondervan Publishing House. All rights reserved.

The prayer on pages 23-24 by James F. Engel, ©1998 by Development Associates International, is used by
permission.

The letter excerpt on pages 134-37 by Oscar Muriu is used by permission.

Cover photograph: Carroll Seghers II/Photo Researchers Inc.

ISBN 0-8308-2239-9

Printed in the United States of America ∞

Library of Congress Cataloging-in-Publication Data

Engel, James F.

    Changing the mind of missions: where have we gone wrong?/ James F. Engel &
William A. Dyrness.

    p. cm.

    Includes bibliographical references.

    ISBN 0-8308-2239-9 (pbk.: alk. paper)

    1. Missions.   I. Dyrness, William A.   II. Title.

BV2063.E535 2000

266—dc21

                                99-088405

19	18	17	16	15	14	13	12	11	10	9	8	7	6	5	4	3	2	1
15	14	13	12	11	10	09	08	07	06	05	04	03	02	01	00			

Contents

Preface

This book was born over a shared lunch some time ago when the authors met while serving on a ministry advisory board. As we recounted our respective pilgrimages in the field of missions, we found that we shared common convictions about the contemporary missions world—though we came from very different backgrounds.

These convictions grow out of two deep concerns. The first is the overriding desire to see the world recognize the lordship of Jesus Christ and the related call of the church to extend that lordship in its missions activities. The second is the worry that Western missions have been seriously compromised by their association with modernity in general and with Western forms of political and economic power in particular.

This book is written then for those involved in Western missions: missionaries (and future missionaries!), missions executives and, equally importantly, pastors and church missions committees. Though our focus is on American missions in particular, we believe that much of what we say will be applicable to missionary agencies worldwide. We do not say this because we believe the future of world missions lies necessarily with this group of people—in many ways we will argue that it does not—but because these groups control extremely important resources and are the stewards of a rich tradition of missions.

We write for them moreover because we treasure this heritage and have been deeply involved with it ourselves over many years. Jim was a marketing educator and practitioner until he became a follower of Jesus in his thirties and found himself in an entirely different world, serving Christian leaders as a teacher and consultant in strategic thinking and leadership development all over the globe. Bill was reared in a Christian home deeply involved in missions, married into a missionary family and became a missionary theologian in the Philippines and Africa, and he is currently serving as a dean at Fuller Seminary. Both of us yearn to see our Western colleagues become better stewards both of the gospel and of their tradition and resources.

We do not want to claim that the points we make are new or original. In many ways we want to recover the heritage and spirit of missions from earlier periods in history, especially as laid out in the New Testament. Indeed throughout our work we have often remembered that Roland Allen made many of the points we make almost one hundred years ago in his classic *Missionary Methods: St. Paul's or Ours.* More recently we acknowledge our debts to David Bosch, Samuel Escobar, Os Guinness, Lesslie Newbigin, René Padilla, Andrew Walls and Mark Noll, among others. We have sought to build on the shoulders of these writers.

Nor do we want to sound a pessimistic note—indeed we believe there is genuine reason for optimism. As we have noted, there has recently been much writing and rethinking of missions that calls us to reform our methods and structures in ways that are helpful. Most encouraging, the impetus of world missions is gradually being picked up by Christians from the younger churches who have a different heritage and fresh cultural expectations. Since we are writing for a Western audience and dealing with problems particular to them, we make only selected reference to these growing non-Western efforts; a full treatment of these would require a separate book and a different focus. But we venture to suggest that many of the problems they face are similar.

This book seeks to respond to the need, as we see it, to return to the biblical ground on which Jesus walked as he established and extended his kingdom on earth. We are united in the conviction that the West perpetuates a virtual strategic juggernaut on the world, which seriously distorts the Great Commission. Our intent in these pages is to address these distortions forthrightly and to demonstrate the extent to which Western efforts have fallen short of the mark. But we also have endeavored to address the practical issues of what must be done to restore biblical fidelity and wisdom to the cause of world missions.

We wish to thank those who have read portions of the manuscript and offered their critical comments. We acknowledge especially Paul Borthwick, David Fraser, Max Meyers, Luis Bush, Jane Overstreet, Doug Sparks, David Kasali and Karla Riggs Norton. We also want to acknowledge the encouragement of colleagues Paul McKaughan and Jim Plueddemann.

It has been a pleasure to work with InterVarsity Press, especially with our senior editor Dan Reid, who has understood and affirmed from the outset everything we are trying to do. Such empathy and expertise is rare and much appreciated. We also acknowledge the efficient and responsive support received from Fuller's office of Academic Publications, especially Alex Pak, Susan Wood and Ann White.

Finally, to our wives, Sharon and Grace, thanks for encouraging us in this joint venture. Thanks to both of you for bearing with us with patience and understanding. This book is dedicated to you.

James F. Engel, Philadelphia, Pennsylvania
William A. Dyrness, Pasadena, California

1

············

A Clouded Future?

A long day is finally drawing to a close.[1] *Bud Anderson sits back in* his office chair feeling weary as he contemplates the board meeting set to begin over dinner that night. It seems like an eternity since he was called from field leadership to the position of President of Global Harvest Mission [a fictitious name]. *Every year it's the same old thing,* he thinks, *barely breaking even financially and stretching every way we can just to keep alive.*

GHM was founded in 1947 as a nondenominational agency of evangelical tradition engaged in church planting and evangelism. It grew rapidly at the beginning under the leadership of its dynamic founder, Dr. Ralph Carpenter, who died a few years ago. Staff growth has slowed, however, with a present total of forty-nine missionary families serving in eleven fields on two continents, only a slight increase over previous years.

Bud had little idea of what was to happen when he stepped into Dr. Carpenter's shoes. He was excited then about using his gifts of motivation and encouragement to serve the missionaries and national church leaders worldwide. What he did not expect, however, was to spend nearly 60 percent of his time simply keeping the agency alive through fundraising and financial oversight.

Well, at least we avoided a deficit this year, he says to himself after contemplating the grim memory of two straight years of borrowing from reserves and restricted fund accounts. He is anything but optimistic, however, that the current year's budget of $12,058,000 can be met without some heroic efforts. *I'm not a fundraiser,* he thinks, *but what choice do I have?* Bud's sense of anxiety grows as he contemplates the prospect of seemingly endless church presentations and donor visits crowding his schedule in the coming months.

In the thirty minutes remaining Bud reflects on the changes that have taken place since he and his wife, Carol, joined GHM as first-term missionaries straight out of seminary in 1972. *It wasn't any problem raising support back then. It seemed as though everyone was interested in overseas missions and glad to help out.* He can't help remembering the enthusiasm with which Carol and he were received by their supporters and home church on furloughs. And the others who came aboard in that decade had the same experience. *That was a great time in which to be a missionary.*

The glow of that memory fades sharply, however, as the time of the board meeting draws close. Bud cannot help reflecting back on his latest visit just a few days ago to a long-time supporting congregation, the First Church of Rollingwood. He finds himself crying out, "Lord, what has happened? It's the same old story. I practically had to beg to get inside the door, and then what did I find? The usual excuse that 'missions falls way down on the list of priorities.'

"The only people interested at all in missions are those my age or older. Most of the others have closed their eyes to a world beyond their own home and neighborhood, and nothing we do seems to make any difference. What's it going to take, Lord, to shake them out of their lethargy?"

The only thing that provides him any encouragement is the fact that growing numbers in their twenties express real concerns about victims of unrighteousness around the world.

Bud has had to face the discouraging fact that the "romance of missions" that captivated previous generations is almost a thing of the past. Everyone at GHM is discouraged by the growing number of months—and even years—it takes a new missionary to raise support, to say nothing of the fact that the funds needed to put an American family on the field are nearly prohibitive.

GHM has experienced, along with all missions agencies, a growing interest in short-term missions within the local church, but this raises an altogether different set of issues. Especially troubling is the fact that there has been a sharp decrease in the numbers who are willing to go out as career missionaries. "What are we to become," Bud cries out, "just an outlet for yet another youth ministry program?"

Fortunately GHM has had some success in raising project funds, but this too has been a mixed blessing. Development director Rick Henley finally has been forced to admit, "Just about everybody seems to be interested in getting more 'bang for the buck' in the money they give, and our ministry doesn't seem to excite them as it once did." The Muslim ministry in one restricted and highly resistant country, in particular, has languished because of inability to cite the numbers of converts that donors seem to expect.

Bud's sense of burden becomes even greater, however, as he reviews the growth of the GHM-affiliated church on the field around the world. While he praises God for the increase in numbers of converts and indigenous leadership, he cannot ignore the fact that missionaries no longer are needed or wanted to play the pioneering role they once did. His greatest concern is with the twenty-one missionary couples over the age of fifty who went to the field in totally different times and now find themselves caught in the trap of a mission that to a high degree has "worked itself out of a job." Bud's daily prayer is, "Oh Lord, how can I help them?"

Finally, and perhaps most difficult to face, is Bud's growing doubts on the long-term effectiveness of the majority of GHM's programs, which in recent years have increasingly been focused on accelerating the pace of evangelism on its fields. While the number of converts has been increasing, sometimes even dramatically, there does not seem to be much impact on the surrounding community. He has to agree sadly with African leader Phineas Dubé who has observed that the church on his continent and in the world is "twenty miles wide and one inch deep." "Lord," Bud prays, "shouldn't we be seeing change in rapidly deteriorating morality, poverty and quality of life?" Sadly, he has come to recognize that these fruits of a truly redeemed life are not being experienced on a wide scale.

There is no question in Bud's mind that storm clouds are gathering that imperil the very future of GHM and many other agencies that face these changes. "What am I going to say at this meeting, Lord? What is our future if it keeps going on in this way?"

Fortunately, Bud will soon discover that the spark for innovation and change exists in both his staff and board that will transform GHM from an agency functioning within the paradigms of yesterday to one that will regain its lost cutting edge. Nevertheless, the process of change will be a challenging one.

What Bud has no way of knowing is that a similar sense of despair is being felt by the missions committee leaders in First Church of Rollingwood and others like it, which are listing in the waters of change and facing a serious erosion in missions interest and support.

Sally Calderone and her husband, George, have been members of First Church of Rollingwood since the middle 1970s, with Sally now in her tenth year as chairperson of the missions committee. On the very evening that Bud Anderson faces harsh realities, she convenes her monthly committee meeting. After an opening prayer the first topic of business is the request from Bud Anderson for a $10,000 grant to fund two national evangelists in southern Africa.

Sally has great hesitation in forwarding such a request at this point, even though two GHM missionaries have been supported for many years by First Church. A positive response seems most unlikely to her given the message from a newly arrived and disappointed Senior Pastor Geoff Finch that the missions fund has to be cut once again to balance the budget.

To her, Bud is oblivious to the missions realities in supporting congregations such as First Church. He should be aware that First Church in these early days of Geoff's pastorate is far different than it was in the 1970s when it first began to support GHM under the leadership of Pastor Tom Bartlett. That was the time in which the church grew rapidly both in numbers and in quality of spiritual life, spearheaded through a focus on individual discipleship and community life in small groups. Outreach both to the community and to the world burgeoned as creative ways were found to turn lay interest and initiative into a congregational reality. In fact, nearly one third of the budget went to world missions.

But a succession of pastors who followed Tom somehow failed to continue to unleash the resources of First Church in this dramatic way. Attendance grew for a while, particularly through inauguration of what came to be known as a "seeker-sensitive" worship service. But somehow church attendance did not extend very far into congregational involvement as it did in earlier years. In short, First Church became yet another stop on the church-shopping circuit—plateaued in growth, outwardly successful but increasingly barren of impact beyond its walls.

At this point, missions interest has virtually collapsed at First Church, a largely baby-boom-aged congregation. Widespread skepticism is expressed throughout the church on the need for missions any longer given the growth of the church in the Two-Thirds World. And many otherwise committed evangelicals openly question, albeit cautiously, whether Jesus is the only way to God, given the growth of Islam and other religions. Not surprisingly, the budget for world missions has dropped over the years to less than 12 percent of the total.

But Sally's reservations are deeper. Bud did not take the time to learn that she and George returned less than a year ago from a dynamic three month involvement with another mission that literally changed their lives. While on the field with others they were immersed in daily Bible study and individual discipleship accompanied by a thorough grounding in crosscultural ministry skills. During the remaining time they partnered with national leaders in helping some of the most destitute to start small businesses. Before long, interest began to develop in neighborhood Bible studies, and word was just received that a church has been planted where they lived and worked.

A spark seemed to ignite on their return as they shared this with a few friends and small-group members. Suddenly three other couples had the vision that First Church could do far more than just send funds overseas and, to Sally's delight, her missions committee doubled from six to twelve members, including one couple in their twenties. Pastor Geoff is elated and promises to make this his top priority as he assumes this new pastorate. Together they began to realize that the church itself can be creatively involved in a field ministry of its own through partnerships of this kind with churches and nationals.

In short, First Church is experiencing the first spark that could lead it from a passive missions church to one that is creative and proactive in helping the kingdom and reign of God grow on this earth. What the committee needs at this time is help and guidance from existing missions such as GHM as they embark tentatively and perhaps naively on a challenging new venture. Instead, in Sally's eyes what they have received is yet another request to funnel money beyond their walls to a missions board that is facing its own effectiveness crisis.

Bud's request for funds is denied, and it is likely that future appeals will fall on barren ground. GHM is totally unprepared to cope with a church that is about to move out of the doldrums of passive missions support in the form of personnel and funds.

Fortunately, as we will see in coming pages, the opportunity for a creative partnership between GHM and Rollingwood church has not been lost.

* * *

SO HERE WE HAVE IT—A MISSIONS AGENCY AND A SUPPORTING church both mired in an effectiveness crisis. While GHM and First Church of Rollingwood are fictitious, there is no denying the fact the dilemma both face is to one degree or another experienced in many churches and agencies.[2] North American contribution to world missions indeed does face a clouded future. Nevertheless, the spark for change exists within both churches and agencies. The starting point is growing recognition that something has seriously gone wrong with the harvest—the world has changed, whereas the church and its agencies, to a disturbing degree, continue to act as if nothing has changed. As James Engel put it:

> North American Christian commitment to world evangelization is in sharp retrenchment. Unless there is an intervention by God leading to across-the-board willingness in churches and agencies to cope with changing paradigms and realities, North America will become a secondary force in the world church.[3]

Coming to Grips with Changing Realities
The purpose of this book is to help you understand why this crisis has arisen and what it will take to reverse the dangerous sag and decline now so disturbingly evident. Both authors are veterans on the world scene, with wide experience in many countries of the world with churches and agencies. While we grieve over this current slump, this book is motivated by a joint, heartfelt desire to see the missions enterprise function in the way God intended and for it to prosper once again.

The North American missions movement is facing realities amazingly similar to those confronting American industry for nearly twenty years. Almost overnight a more nimble and highly competitive Japanese industrial juggernaut almost overwhelmed its sluggish counterparts worldwide. An all-new information-oriented approach to production, marketing and management suddenly was forced upon enterprises that somehow had ignored the unmistakable signs of change on the horizon. Few industries were left untouched by an immediate imperative to adapt and change or die! Fortunately, corporate boards and management saw the handwriting on the wall and responded with a startling degree of courage and brilliance.

Similarly ominous signs have been on the world missions horizon for more than two decades, but it seems to take much longer for churches and Christian organizations to recognize realities. And when the light finally dawns, the response all too often is to bury our heads in the sand, trusting that God somehow will make things right.

The time has passed for that kind of sluggish stewardship. It is time to come to grips with three unmistakable trends threatening to derail all that remains of a once potent world missions thrust:

1. The contemporary missions movement is too often captive to American cultural realities, associating the gospel with economic and political pragmatism.

2. Meanwhile, the initiative in missions has shifted to the younger churches.

3. Most seriously, missions has frequently lost sight of its theological roots by reducing the gospel to proclamation.

An Evangelical Church Losing Its Power and Influence

A generation of baby boomer Christians (those born between 1946 and 1965) now controls the destiny of the North American church, and this certainly is the case at First Church of Rollingwood. And a younger generation is coming along with its own questions and priorities. It is, of course, dangerous to generalize about any given generation, but there are some widespread, pervasive lifestyle characteristics:

☐ Individualism. Life is characterized by a search for meaning, fulfillment and self-gratification as this generation questions the values of earlier generations.

☐ Pluralism. Most under the age of forty have much wider latitudes and tolerance for diversity. The legalism and rigidity of previous generations is questioned and abandoned. While this is a healthy trend in many respects, there is real danger that the historical doctrinal foundations of Christianity may be weakened in an atmosphere of tolerance.

☐ Skepticism. Existing institutions, especially traditionally focused churches and missions, are subjected to a searchlight of relevance, and many are found wanting.

☐ Activism. Boomers will tackle issues and seek for solutions when they are equipped and motivated to do so. They are highly selective, however, in their priorities and focus mostly on causes directly affecting them.

☐ Isolationism. There is little tolerance for efforts that appear to be throwing resources at world needs that seem to defy solution. Hence, world missions is pushed to the very bottom of their priorities.

While worshiping numbers have maintained a historical trend at about 40 percent of the population on a given Sunday, the North American church, other than for a frequently vocal and active Christian right, has diverted its attention from its society and world to a quest to be "seeker sensitive." It aims to increase worship attendance by addressing and satisfying felt needs. While this is legitimate as a partial strategy, the outcome is a church, with admittedly notable exceptions, drawn in upon itself, concentrating on management of its programs, characterized by a depletion of passion for causes beyond its own perimeters.

For these reasons, there is an effectiveness crisis at First Church of Rollingwood. Fortunately, there is a younger generation in their twenties and thirties motivated by a very different outlook that is just beginning to exert its influence in ways that will make a real difference as we will discover in coming pages.

In a landmark survey of giving patterns in mainline Protestant and evangelical churches, John and Sylvia Ronsvalle discovered that giving for benevolent causes (anything beyond the inner life of the congregation) decreased by more than one third between 1969 and 1993.[4] If this decline were to continue at that pace, all benevolent giving would approach zero in the middle of the twenty-first century! To compound this dilemma even further, missions usually ranks at the very bottom of baby boom priorities in charitable and religious contributions.[5]

The outcome, quite logically, is that most sending agencies are facing a financial crisis that seriously curbs any significant initiatives to capitalize upon missions opportunities.[6]

Mission agencies are pressed to find more "effective" methods to do their work in ways that are more cost-effective. An unfortunate result is that methods and plans often seem to drive programs more than do biblical principles.

A Shift of Missions Leadership and Momentum to the Two-Thirds World Church

Many are shocked to learn that a majority of missionaries in the world now come from the Two-Thirds World. The truth is that power, leadership and influence in world missions circles have been shifting for several decades away from North America and Europe to the point that the most exciting initiatives in missions have a profoundly different geographical focus.

In the very best sense, this is cause for celebration because the baby has now become a vigorous, maturing and responsible adult in many parts of Africa, Asia and South America.

But what does this development mean for a missions enterprise that still announces its primary focus to be pioneering crosscultural evangelism and church planting in the time-honored way? There seems to be an unwarranted assumption that a Western expatriate can somehow perform the task as well or better than those who are much closer geographically, linguistically and culturally.

The view that we have gleaned from a large number of Two-Thirds World leaders presents quite a different perspective:

☐ A strong Western presence inhibits development of indigenous resources, both people and funding, and maintains an unhealthy dependence on the outside.

☐ Too many agencies launch programs and initiatives that are conceived in the West and then recruit local support and involvement.

Not surprisingly, such efforts more often than not prove to be inappropriate and even harmful in other contexts. Though well-intended, the efforts once again often curb the initiatives of the indigenous church and perpetuate the longstanding image of Western domination.

☐ There is widespread concern over the marked hesitation of the Western missions movement to join in the struggle of the indigenous church and its agencies to integrate evangelism and social transformation following the example of Jesus. As chapter three will make clear, we have too long perpetuated a Western privatized faith on the field that dichotomizes evangelism and social transformation in a destructive way. As a result, pragmatics have replaced theological reflection and biblical obedience.

The door is slowly but steadily swinging shut on North Americans who are reluctant to recognize that the Two-Thirds World and its churches now lie at the very center of world missions influence and initiative. The need now is to come alongside in a spirit of partnership and submission, participating where we can in an enabling and facilitating manner to help increase the impact of all that God is doing in this era. For this to happen GHM, First Church of Rollingwood and other churches and agencies must shift gears and change directions in a decisive way. We will have much to say on this issue in coming chapters.

Loss of the Full Biblical Context of the Great Commission

Christ's command to "go and make disciples of all the nations," appearing in Matthew 28:18-20, has long been cited as the marching order for his church. From the very beginning of the Bible, starting in the twelfth chapter of Genesis, we see that God is a *missionary God* whose intent is to show his goodness to all mankind in all ages. The expectation is that God's people will be willing participants.

What has Christ asked us to do? Our contention is that this call has been interpreted for many decades, especially in North America and parts of Western Europe, as *communicating a set of biblical propositions to a maximum number of people and declaring them as "reached" once this takes place.* In other words, go, evangelize, plant churches, and measure success by *numerical response!*

This agenda has dutifully been propagated during this century by well-meaning missionaries to the point that it has come to dominate outreach strategies of the church around the globe. It is being expressed today by accelerated evangelism in the form of donor-developed strategic plans designed to sow the word of God everywhere, preferably before the start of a new millennium. And it has been successful—if we are to believe current statistics. Ninety-three percent of the world presumably has been evangelized, and our missions task allegedly is virtually completed.[7]

There is no question that the Christian presence indeed is being expanded globally. But is *evangelism* the outcome Christ intended when he said, "Go and make disciples of all nations, baptizing them in the name of the Father and of the Son and of the Holy Spirit, and teaching them to obey everything I have commanded you" (Mt 28:19-20)? Making disciples involves much more than encouraging people to accept certain truths about God and to begin attending church. It involves a total transformation of the heart and life that involves a righteousness that impacts not only individuals but families, communities and nations. We have much more to say on this subject in chapter two.

For a number of reasons explained in chapter three, Western Christians must plead guilty, first of all, to the charge leveled by Dallas Willard of *a great omission in the Great Commission* through evangelism largely devoid of spiritual formation that "prepares God's people for works of service" (Eph 4:12).[8] In short, we have to a disturbing degree missed the full richness of the Great Commission by our single-minded focus on evangelism. A respected Christian leader in Francophone Africa declared with the enthusiastic amen of many others that "you missionaries brought us Christ but never taught us how to live."

Equally serious is a Western cultural worldview that, from the time of the Enlightenment (see chapter three), relegates faith largely to the private and personal areas of individual life and flees from the problems of the world into fascination with inner spiritual life.[9]

What a contrast with the life and words of Jesus who called us to join him in the process of extending the present realities of the kingdom of God—his lordship over all of life—throughout the world. Consider carefully what Christ said when he announced the "mission statement" for his life: "The Spirit of the Lord is on me, because he anointed me to preach good news to the poor. He has sent me to proclaim freedom for the prisoners and recovery of sight for the blind, to release the oppressed, to proclaim the year of the Lord's favor" (Lk 4:18-19). If this defines his agenda, it also must define ours. No fractured worldview here, confining faith to one's individual and personal life. Rather, there is a bold mandate to combine faith with action to overcome injustice and oppression.

This cultural captivity of the Great Commission is having shattering effects. Who can ignore the debacle of Rwanda, a country often cited in the early 1990s as our best success story in Western world missions? Rwanda, a country where 80 percent claimed to be Christian, engaged in a carnage unparalleled in modern times—a carnage and bloodbath often led by Christians! How could such a tragedy happen in such a beautiful East African country with so much promise?[10] There now is broad agreement on the following root causes:

☐ Christianity was little more than a superficial, privatized veneer on a secular lifestyle characterized by animistic values and longstanding tribal hatred and warfare.

☐ A controlling top-down style of leadership succeeded in building large churches but largely neglected the hard work of unleashing people and building disciples who could be active participants following the reign of Christ in his world.

☐ The church was silent on such critical life-and-death issues as the dignity and worth of each person made in the image of God.

☐ The church relied on outside financial resources, which had created a debilitating dependence.

But we do not have to turn to the Two-Thirds World to see the outcome. How we can justify a virtually silent church throughout the West—an inward-drawn, privatized religion—in an era characterized by a downward spiral of morals, a growing gap between the rich and the poor, an increasingly hazardous environment, spiraling crime, financial manipulation, business and political corruption, and widespread lack of genuine hope?

A Call for Biblical Fidelity

It is our contention, then, that the missions momentum from North America and much of the remaining Western world is functioning within theological paradigms and resulting ministry practices dating back prior to the dawn of the twentieth century. The only hope for change is to start once again with the agenda of a *missionary God*, expressed through the life and words of his Son. In short, we must define the modern realities of the Lordship and reign of Christ in a crumbling world. Unless our missions enterprise is constructed on this biblical foundation, we build in vain!

Furthermore, now is the time for commonsense recognition of changing world realities. What justification can be given for missionary-sending practices dating back to the turn of the twentieth century when the Two-Thirds World church has now assumed the leadership and momentum in such a clear and powerful way?

It is our objective in this book, first of all, to diagnose further what has gone wrong with the harvest. It is not our intent to be negative, but we must break lose from the peril of outmoded ways of thinking. In fact, our message will be an exceedingly positive and encouraging one. We truly believe that we are on the very brink of unparalleled revival and change. Can we afford to be left behind as the rest of the world moves on? Please join us in this prayer.

A Prayer For Renewal and Restoration

Heavenly father, our Lord and giver of life, forgive us—
for the extent to which we have naively succumbed to the spirit of the age,
for our preoccupation with false measures of success,
for a sense of triumphalism which replaces humble dependence on you,
and for our blindness in avoiding those parts of your word which do not fit neatly into our theology.
We humbly confess our total dependence on you as the Lord of life.
Let us see a lost world afresh through your eyes
and give us discernment through your spirit.

Share with us your priorities,
and give us the courage to be responsible stewards
of our obligation to take the whole gospel to the whole world.
Speak, Lord, for your servants are listening.
To you we give all glory, honor, and praise
in the name of the Father, the Son, and the Holy Spirit.[11]

2

. . . .

Where in the World
Is Jerusalem?

Sally Calderone and her missions committee at First Church of Roll-
ingwood are about to embark on quite an adventure. Under the
leadership of Pastor Geoff Finch, the entire committee agreed to
meet weekly to discover together what the Bible has to say
about "God as a missionary God." They also were joined by fellow church member James Morey, regional representative for
the Global Harvest Mission. Together they will move through
the teachings of Jesus Christ in the Gospels as well as the missions experiences in the first century as documented in the book
of Acts.

This group of committed seekers is about to discover the revolutionary truth that world missions goes well beyond its predominant contemporary expression as accelerated evangelism
to "reach the unreached." Little by little their eyes will be
opened to the revolutionary truth that Christian missions is the
announcement, embodiment and extension of Christ's reign in

the world, by the power of the Holy Spirit to the glory of the Father.

In other words, they will encounter a Jesus Christ whose appearance constituted what G. K. Chesterton called that blow against the backbone of history, that earthshaking event that transformed all of creation and inaugurated his reign on earth that the New Testament calls the "new creation" (2 Cor 5:17). In the process they will become acutely aware that the church today too often functions as a vast clerical machinery producing a complacent, individualized and often impotent form of Christianity that gives little evidence of the sweeping power of Christ's reign in this world. It will not take long to discover that the only avenue to restoration is a return to the times of Jesus to recover a sharpened vision of what it really means to take the gospel from "Jerusalem to Judea and to the ends of the world."

* * *

STANDING AT THE END OF TWO MILLENNIA OF CHRISTIAN HISTORY, it is difficult for us to comprehend the world in which the church was born. We are so used to seeing Jesus and the disciples honored in the splendor of cathedrals and altarpieces that we forget the modest and unremarkable beginnings of the Christian movement. During the time the New Testament was written, the church was probably made up, at most, of a few thousand believers, mostly from humble backgrounds, scattered in small congregations throughout the sprawling Roman Empire. Though small, it soon experienced division between parties that attached themselves to particular leaders and represented differing attitudes toward its Jewish ancestry.

To say the church had little political and economic influence would be an understatement. Paul insists on pointing out how few of the Corinthians were powerful or of noble birth (1 Cor 1:26). Moreover, the church competed with a wide variety of religious movements and with a Judaism that was itself divided and unsure of its future. Christians soon experienced opposition not only from the more orthodox Jews but also from the Roman authorities.

As the final indignity, Jerusalem was undergoing persistent peri-

ods of economic distress and famine that exacerbated the unjust
social structure of the empire. In short, the world of the first century
was, in many ways, a world much like our own! The small struggling Christian movement faced enormous challenges. What then
accounts for the enormous attraction and impact of a Christian
movement with such inauspicious beginnings? How do we account
for the fact that in a little over two centuries it went from being an
outlawed religion to being the dominant religion of the empire?

The answer is found in one pivotal event: *the appearance of Jesus
Christ as God's messiah to inaugurate the last days of God's reign on earth
and to call out a people to announce and embody that reign.* The Gospels
are filled with ringing announcements that must have shocked a
complacent religious world. Jesus' teaching and miracles were so
remarkable that wherever he went he gathered a crowd and even
succeeded in persuading a small number to follow him as disciples.

Some of these early followers later wrote down things he had
done and said. They remembered the earthshaking announcement,
"The time has come. . . . The kingdom of God is near. Repent and
believe the good news" (Mk 1:15). This striking call so distinguished
Jesus from other religious teachers that it required either a life-
changing confession or conscious opposition.

In the Gospel of Luke, Jesus' opening announcement of his mission is, if anything, even more far-reaching. At his own hometown
he rose dramatically in the synagogue and dared to apply the hal-
lowed messianic prophecy of Isaiah to himself. As we pointed out in
chapter one, the divine mission for Jesus was captured in these
words: "The Spirit of the Lord is on me, because he has anointed me
to preach good news to the poor. He has sent me to proclaim freedom for the prisoners and recovery of sight for the blind, to release
the oppressed, to proclaim the year of the Lord's favor" (Lk 4:18-19
quoting from Is 61:1-2 and 58:6). This day has now come, Jesus
insisted. And the audience showed how clearly it understood the
implications of what he was saying by taking him out of the city
onto the brow of a hill and seeking to throw him down headlong!

This message then and now calls for nothing less than a complete
(and sacrificial) commitment of our whole life and the subsequent

transformation of all our ways of thinking and living. In short, we are called—then and now—to be his *disciples*. Little wonder that the number of those who actually followed Jesus was small, and even these chosen few often misunderstood the extent of the demands he was making. Division and spiritual immaturity in the early church blunted Christ's call to discipleship. And yet, despite their small numbers and imperfections, consider the impact of this small band of people on the Roman world!

This has always been God's way with his people—taking Abraham, Ruth, Amos and Peter—ordinary people—and using these flawed vessels as vehicles of his glory. As David Bosch put it: "Throughout most of the church's history its empirical state has been deplorable. This was already true of Jesus' first circle of disciples and has not really changed since."[1] Nonetheless the expansion of the church throughout its two-thousand-year history has left an indelible, totally unique mark in the form of economic lift among the poor, social and political justice, and Christian living characterized by integrity and holiness.[2]

God delights in taking the few who respond, whatever their background and gifts, and shaping them into a community through which he penetrates the social order in powerful ways. For, Paul says, "God chose what is foolish in the world to shame the wise, what is weak in the world to shame the strong, what is low and despised in the world, even things that are not, to bring to nothing the things that are" (1 Cor 1:27-28).

To help us recover our bearings in missions, we need to spend some time reflecting on the mandates Jesus gave to his disciples who were told to carry on his mission and reign in this world. What is it really that God asks his people to do and be? Once this is clarified, we will use that lens to evaluate what the contemporary world church is doing to carry this mission onward as we enter the third millennium. We will see that Western missions needs to experience a reorientation of its thinking and practice—to see the broader scope of Christ's reign, and the growing diversity of missions opportunities. Jerusalem is no longer only in the West; rather there are now many Jerusalems from which God's Word is spreading.

The Mission as Given by Jesus

What is clear from Jesus' instructions to his disciples at the end of his life is that he envisioned a wide variety of situations in which "missions" would be carried out. If we count the promise in the first chapter of Acts as a separate account from that in Luke (though written by the same person), we have five different kinds of instructions for missions, all together making up a comprehensive and suggestive picture of the Christian's work in the world.

The Gospel of Matthew. We begin with Matthew's version of what has come to be known as the *Great Commission* (though this phrase does not appear in Scripture). Matthew is a very Jewish Gospel that portrays Jesus as the new Moses, the new lawgiver who goes up on the mountain and speaks words from God. Matthew treats the Old Testament with great respect but, amazingly, puts the teachings of Jesus on a par with those of Moses. "You have heard that it was said, but I tell you. . ." is the common form of Jesus' teaching in the Sermon on the Mount (Mt 5—7). Both the teaching of the Old Testament and Jesus' own teaching converge on the path that leads Jesus to the cross and the subsequent vindication of his ministry in the resurrection.

The instructions at the end of chapter 28, then, are meant to be the climax of both the resurrection narrative and the book as a whole. The context is a mountain in Galilee (where Matthew had also begun his description of Jesus' ministry) to which Jesus had directed the disciples. Why would Jesus want to meet his disciples here in Galilee, which was considered the most provincial part of Palestine? Little wonder the disciples were confused about the meaning of all this; some were skeptical, others worshiped him. In the midst of this uncertainty, Jesus gave his parting command.

This command begins and ends with a promise. First he recalls something that has been a central theme of Matthew's Gospel: "All authority in heaven and on earth has been given to me." This becomes the ground on which all the work of Christians is carried out: Jesus' cosmic lordship, which is based on his death and resurrection. "Therefore," Jesus goes on, "you are to . . . make disciples." Notice that in spite of all the missionary sermons we have heard (and most translations), the command is not actually about going somewhere; *it is about making disciples.* Jesus says literally, "As you go, make disciples of all nations." Or better for a people like us who are always on the go: "Wherever you go, *do my work* and make disciples of (or in) all the nations."

This may not mean going farther than to our next-door neighbor. The object of our mission is not people "over there" but all people everywhere—all need to become disciples or followers of Jesus. It is not about going out to reach people but our reaching out to people to bring them to Jesus. This is a vital theme in Matthew's Gospel. Disciples are called, as Donald Hagner puts it, "to follow after righteousness as articulated in the teaching of Jesus."[3]

The process of disciple making is further described by the instruction to baptize and teach all that Jesus commanded. What this means is that people from all nations are to be brought into the fellowship of believers and instructed in ways that bring them to maturity in Christ. This is of course more than a simple sharing of information; it is imparting the powerful presence of Christ himself. This invocation of Christ's presence is supported by the final promise of verse 20: "I am with you always, to the very end of the age." This is not only a major claim to Christ's divinity but a reiteration of the theological meaning of Christ's life as Matthew portrays it: Christ is Emmanuel—*God with us.*

So the instructions that end this Gospel focus almost exclusively on the presence and the authority (power) of the resurrected Christ. Disciple making, in a wonderful and mysterious sense, is *an extension of that divine presence.* The fact of our "going" is the subordinate reality, because Christ's authority precedes and empowers our efforts. We are simply called to urge people from among all the nations *(ethnic groups)* to become faithful followers of Christ.

Notice two implications of this for our understanding of missions today. The first is that the object of missions activity is the whole world, all nations. As Jesus put it in Matthew 13:38, "the field is the world" in which the sower sows. There is no hint whatsoever that it is divided into areas that are missions fields (the periphery) and others that are not (the center).

All peoples are now called to accountability to the lordship of the risen Christ. This leads to the second major implication for missions. *The power and authority for missions comes wholly and exclusively from the risen Christ who calls his church to serve him.* In case we might miss the full impact of this, Jesus stresses that all authority in heaven and on earth belongs to him by right. Do not lose the impact of this statement: all lesser authority (political, cultural and economic) has been called to account in light of this new ruler, the King of Kings.

The Gospel of Mark. When we turn to the Gospel of Mark a new element is added to Jesus' final words to his disciples. If Matthew's stress is on *teaching* what Jesus' taught and embodied, Mark's stress is on *preaching the good news.* In fact, Mark records in his first chapter that both John and Jesus "proclaim" the good news of the kingdom of God, which is being fulfilled in Jesus' life and ministry. This good news is demonstrated by the mighty acts of the master—the authoritative defeat of Satan, the forgiveness of sins, healing the sick, feeding the hungry and raising the dead. And it is climaxed in Jesus' own death and resurrection, the account of which takes up more than a third of the book.

As in Matthew, *discipleship* is critical for Mark. He goes out of his way to portray the consistent failure of the disciples to understand what Jesus was saying and to show Jesus' attempts to get them to understand (see Mk 8:21). In fact, according to a recent argument, Mark viewed discipleship as a conversion process in and of itself taking place over a lifetime.[4] And (if you accept the longer ending of Mark as authentic)[5] it is a process that culminates in Jesus' command to continue his work of announcing the arrival of the kingdom (see Mk 16:15-18).

Again after his resurrection appearances in Mark 16:9-13 he appears to his disciples and upbraids them for their lack of faith. Three times in a few verses their unbelief is underlined (vv. 11, 13, 14). But in spite of the many failures of these unpromising candidates, he calls them to "preach the good news to all creation " (v. 15). Here the stress is on the announcement of the good news to all God's creation throughout the whole world, rather than on disciple making. Those who respond, verse 16 goes on to say, will be saved, and those who do not will be condemned.

It is interesting to note that Mark's Gospel is the nearest equivalent in Scripture to a call to evangelize the world—the great theme of today's missions movement as the third millennium is about to begin. But the scope of the activity is broadened to include all that God has made (the word refers not simply to the human creature but all of creation). This dimension, consistent with Matthew's stress on Christ's authority over all in heaven and on earth, is further illustrated by the signs that Christ promises will accompany those who believe: exorcism, tongues, protection against harm (even that associated with deadly snakes) and gifts of healing. Clearly the powers of the kingdom include a renewal of all creation and a victory over all evil powers that would seek to destroy that creation.

So Mark complements Matthew by highlighting the announcement of the state of affairs brought about by Jesus' life, death and resurrection. This new reality, called in Mark the "kingdom of God," has implications not only for all people as in Matthew but all of creation (and culture). God, in Jesus, has reestablished his righteous rule over all creation, not just the souls of his followers, and it is this rule his disciples are to announce and extend everywhere. All human perspectives on authority and power (and on development) are now put into a new and larger perspective.

The Gospel of Luke. Mark fills in a bit the picture that Matthew sketches, but something is still missing: How is all of this going to be possible for the modest band of Jesus' followers? This question begins to be addressed by Luke in his narrative of Jesus' journey from Galilee to Jerusalem. Though written for a Gentile audience, Luke, like Matthew, stresses that Jesus suffered and was raised according to the Old Testament Scriptures. But Luke adds that this Messiah, promised by the Old Testament prophets, is now made Lord of all peoples (including Gentiles). Jesus' saving work in Luke actually inaugurates the kingdom by delivering sinners, forgiving sins and—something not stressed in the other Gospels—sending his Spirit.

Once again after the resurrection appearances to the women and the disciples on the road to Emmaus, Jesus appears in the midst of his disciples while they are puzzling over the meaning of these events (Lk 24:36). In this version he begins with the reminder that everything written about him must be fulfilled, that the Messiah must suffer and be raised the third day, and that "repentance and forgiveness of sins will be preached in his name to all nations, beginning from Jerusalem" (Lk 24:47).

Here the command becomes a kind of promise that will take place in fulfillment of Scripture. That is, rather than saying to the disciples, "This is what you should do," Jesus instead says, "This is what will happen to you!" Jerusalem serves as the starting point of all these things that will take place, being the location of Jesus' death and resurrection. What then is the role of the disciples? Jesus says simply, "You are witnesses of these things" (v. 48). They are directed to fulfill Christ's promises (and Old Testament prophecies) by simply becoming witnesses—those who give testimony by the lives they live and their willingness to share the hope that is within them. The cost for many would be the loss of their lives.

Like the two disciples on the way to Emmaus, then, all the disciples hurry back to their friends and say (witness!), "The Lord has risen and has appeared to Simon" (Lk 24:34). But something is still missing. God has yet to send what he promised, and for this reason the disciples are urged to "stay in the city until you have been clothed with power from on high" (Lk 24:49). This part of the story is continued in Luke's second volume—the book of Acts. There on the mountain of his ascension Jesus repeats this promise: "You will receive power when the Holy Spirit comes upon you; and you will be my witnesses in Jerusalem, and in all Judea and Samaria, and to the ends of the earth" (Acts 1:8).

Once again the primary calling is to become Jesus' witnesses throughout the earth—the listing of places serves as a kind of outline for events recounted in the book of Acts. Indeed Jesus' words are less a command than a prediction; you *will* be witnesses, sometimes—he might have added—against your own better judgment! As the lives of Paul and others demonstrate, some of the most important advances occurred because of God's providential intervention, as in the scattering of the disciples after Stephen's martyrdom and Paul's witness (in chains) in Rome. In every case, believers took advantage of their situation (and their location) to give a joyful witness to their faith in Christ.

The Gospel of John. In John's Gospel there is a strong emphasis on God's presence in the life and work of Jesus Christ—a presence that is to be continued in the disciples of Jesus. In Christ the light that lights everyone (and everything) has come into the world, becoming flesh and tabernacling among us (Jn 1). In the great "I am" passages, Jesus reiterates his role as the divine agent in creation, giving bread and life and hope to a world that is confused and lost. Then in the final upper-room discourse he promises to send "the Counselor" (Jn 16:7), who will lead the disciples into all truth, and by whom they will do greater works than even Jesus has been able to do (Jn 14:12; 16:13-14). This calling is summed up in the famous words of Jesus to the frightened disciples—huddling in fear in a locked house after the resurrection. He appears suddenly in their midst and says: "Peace be with you. As the Father has sent me, I am sending you. . . . Receive the Holy Spirit" (Jn 20:21-22).

This call to incarnate the reality of God, even as Jesus himself did, is further elaborated in yet another, often overlooked, last instruction in the book of John. It can be argued that John gave an equivalent version of a "Great Commission" in the strange exchange between Jesus and Peter in John 21:15-19. This took place following Jesus' appearances to the women at the tomb and subsequently to his disciples by the sea of Tiberias in Galilee (Jn 21:2). There Jesus gives them some instruction on fishing and prepares breakfast. After breakfast Jesus turns and says to Peter, whose betrayal is fresh in both their memories, "Do you love me more than these?" Three times he repeats the question "Do you truly love me?" and each time Peter insists that he does.

Each time, hearing Peter's response, Jesus says simply, "Feed my lambs," "Take care of my sheep," and "Feed my sheep." In other words, love for Jesus must now be demonstrated by obedience to his call and service to his people.[6] This calling is summed up in Jesus' final command to Peter and by extension to all the disciples: "Follow me" (Jn 21:19). Consistent with Jesus' teaching in John, he is the "good shepherd [who] lays down his life for the sheep" (Jn 10:11), and he calls his disciples to follow his example and feed his sheep. As he put it in 12:26, "Whoever serves me must follow me; and where I am, my servant also will be. My father will honor the one who serves me."

Though seldom understood as an instruction about missions, this poignant exchange between Peter and his Lord may contain the most important element of the Christian's commission. *Here Christ calls those who follow him to be certain that all they do—their "following"—flows from a deep-seated and irrevocable love for the Lord.* In this invitation to love him, and out of that love to serve the world, the Christian is invited into the very trinitarian life of God (cf. Jn 14:11-17).[7] That loving relationship in John does not distance itself from the world but incarnates itself in it and seeks to see realized there works that glorify the Father.

The Big Picture as Given by the Creator

How would missions look if we returned to the model of Jesus and the New Testament? With all the activity and publicity surrounding our contemporary missions activity, it is easy to lose sight of the reality of what missions is about. What is the true motivation for missions? Appearances to the contrary, it is not about selling some spectacular product, eternal life or forgiveness of sins, however wonderful these realities are. Missions flows from the heart of a people who have been transformed by the Holy Spirit and who leave all to follow Christ.

The salvation of all people. Missions primarily and fundamentally is about something that God has done—in creation and the new creation, and something God continues to do through the Holy Spirit's empowering of God's people and the proclamation of the gospel, and something God will bring to conclusion when Jesus returns in glory. That is to say, it is primarily about God and indeed, in the end, something that God does through people who follow Christ. Its activities include preaching, teaching, witnessing and loving service.

Notice that Christ placed a many-sided demand on his disciples—a demand that gathered up and connected all the purposes that God had in creating the world and in calling the nation of Israel as a divine emissary, and that included the fullness of God's trinitarian reality. Enabled by the giving of the Holy Spirit at Pentecost, missions then is *the extension of the mighty work that Christ embodied as he restored God's reign on the earth—atoning for human sin on the cross and conquering sin and death in the resurrection. And it is an anticipation of what God one day will do when Christ returns in glory to renew the earth.* It is God-originated, Christ-centered and Spirit-empowered.

In this century we have made great gains in understanding that Christian missions is fundamentally theological in nature, growing out of the person and character of the triune God. This is often referred to as the *missio Dei* (mission of and by God). The influence of Karl Barth has been decisive for this renewed understanding. He insisted that mission must reflect and extend God's own saving activity if it was to be preserved from the secularizing influences so threatening in the twentieth century.[8]

The understanding of missions as rooted in the being and activity of the triune God has two corollaries. First, *missions grows out of all that God has done in creation and new creation.* And since it has to do ultimately with God and God's purposes, the second corollary is that a complete understanding of missions (and therefore an appropriate missions strategy) must be sensitive to the breadth of God's activities from creation to consummation.

The God we proclaim in Jesus Christ is the Creator and Sustainer of the whole universe and all things in it. God has created out of love so that the creature might worship him and so glorify—or reflect—this divine reality. Paul and many of the early church missionaries emphasized this integral perspective on salvation, often beginning their proclamation with a reminder of God's creative activity (see for example, Acts 17:22-24). The objective was to remind their hearers that this news grows out of God's purposes for the whole earth and all people and thus has implications for the whole of their lives and for all of history. Therefore, no privatized or individualistic faith can do justice to the breadth of God's desire for creation.

The person and work of Jesus Christ. Though related to all that God has done since the beginning of time, *the good news remains tied to the person and work of Jesus Christ.* The cross, resurrection and ascension are so familiar to us that we forget how truly revolutionary this new creation appeared within the first-century Mediterranean world. First and foremost, Christ's work was extended to all peoples of the earth. When Jesus began his ministry, the line between Jews and non-Jews (to say nothing of Greeks and non-Greeks!) was very clear. Hellenistic Jews made some attempts to reach out to the Gentiles, but their aim was sometimes more nationalistic than religious.

A significant portion of the Jewish people longed for liberation from their Roman rulers and called for God's vengeance against their enemies. This is probably one of the reasons that Jesus' hearers tried to kill him in Capernaum after he announced, in Isaiah's words, that the Spirit of the Lord was upon him for the release and deliverance of the oppressed. So far his Jewish audience understood and approved what he was saying—they felt *they* were the oppressed and needy.

But in quoting Isaiah 61:1-2 and 58:6, Jesus pointedly left out the last phrase of 61:2: "and the day of vengeance of our God" to be called down on those who are Israel's enemies. In other words, their hopes for vengeance at that point in time were dashed, because Christ came precisely to transform these parochial attitudes. While he made clear that he came to his own people first, he also came for those outside Israel and, ultimately, to their utter astonishment, for *all* people. Even this was consistent with God's purposes for Israel, for Christ came to restore Israel's role as a light to the nations.

Throughout his entire ministry Jesus demonstrated his love for all humankind by healing the Samaritan leper (Lk 17) and the Syrophoenecian woman (Mk 7). In Matthew he uses the faith of the Roman centurion to illustrate that "many will come from the east and the west and will take their places at the feast with Abraham, Isaac and Jacob in the kingdom of heaven" (Mt 8:11). Though coming from Israel and indeed fulfilling God's purposes for Israel, God in the person of Christ was now doing a work that was to extend beyond Israel's borders and include people from every tongue and nation.

As it was in the beginning, so it continues to be. God is calling out his people, the elect, for the benefit of all people, and in missions we are invited to share in this great work. Indeed anyone involved in missions can testify how often they feel like spectators watching God work in peoples' lives.

A new order related to all creation. The fact that Christ's ministry beyond Israel focused on the healing of illnesses and feeding hungry people reminds us that his work extended to all the ills to which creation had become subject. Sins were forgiven, diseases healed, the hungry and thirsty were satisfied; even the dead were raised. All of this comes to a glorious climax in the resurrection of Jesus from the dead, which ultimately was to signal deliverance from the powers of evil, union with God, forgiveness of sins, new birth, release from bondage to sin, a pouring out of the Holy Spirit on all flesh. Little wonder that Paul can go so far as to summarize this as a "new creation"—and in Colossians 1:15-20 pointedly relates this work of Christ to the original creation. Missions grows out of this new order, this renewed creation, that was inaugurated in the resurrection.

Christ's continuing lordship. Missions announces and extends the reality of Christ's lordship over the earth and the powers of evil. Missions, then, is more than proclamation of Christ's story and a call for belief. It also focuses on what God continues to do in the world. As Ferdinand Hahn argued, the early church was a missionary church from the very beginning.[9] Indeed, as he pointed out, the gospel simply spread, at times almost of its own accord, and the church lived by this spreading.

In other words, missions activity from the beginning focused on the people that God was calling out of the world to reflect his character—the body of Christ. The purpose of this corporate body is to provide through our actions, our words and (hopefully) our unity (Jn 14) the essential evidence that validates that God has sent Christ into the world. Indeed the very purpose of the church is to give the world permission to believe in Christ. As Paul put it:

> We [the church] are to God the aroma of Christ among those who are being saved and those who are perishing. To the one we are the smell of death; to the other, the fragrance of life. And who is equal to such a

task? Unlike so many, we do not peddle the word of God for profit. On the contrary, in Christ we speak before God with sincerity, like men sent from God. (2 Cor 2:15-17)

The future when Christ returns. Finally, the good news has a future dimension that anticipates the consummation of Christ's work when he returns for the final establishment of his kingdom on earth. Joachim Jeremias notes, "The special glory of the missionary endeavor lies in the fact that it is a very palpable part of the final consummation inaugurated at Easter."[10] We have the glorious hope of a new heaven and new earth where righteousness dwells. This link of missions with the return of Christ has often been demonstrated in the history of missions by the zeal represented by those groups who have placed the greatest stress on eschatology.

Is There a Model of Missions in the New Testament?
The final commands of Jesus, taken together, issue in a comprehensive demand that God has placed on believers' lives. Nor is this simply for the professional Christian (indeed the group who followed Christ at the beginning were still in a sorry state of preparation) but for all who would follow him. The call is to make disciples by teaching, baptizing, preaching and above all by witnessing and loving. The power of the Christian movement in the New Testament results from the authority of Christ and the power of the Holy Spirit poured out on his people—from the least to the greatest.

Jerusalem was the beginning of missionary activity, not because of its political and economic importance—indeed it was of little significance in the Roman Empire. Of course, it had great religious significance for the Jewish people as the center of temple worship and the place where God's glory dwelt. But as we have hinted, Christ came to reinterpret, indeed to deconstruct, that notion of "center." Jerusalem was important primarily because something happened there that changed the course not only of that time and place but of all times and places. A rule was initiated by Christ's death, resurrection and the pouring out of the Holy Spirit that included the whole earth in its purview. The temple that was to be constructed by this Spirit did not depend on Jerusalem or any other cult center.

For the most part, those who were seized by this rule initially did not belong to the power structures and more often felt like observers to the spread of the gospel than agents.[11] The church was the mission; it did not simply have a mission. The new realities of Christ's redemptive rule first were demonstrated by their lives. As "have-nots" and outcasts their quality of life characterized by sacrifice and love was compelling. They never strayed, at least at the outset, in their opposition to the bonds of unrighteousness and injustice, which were as rampant then as they are today. And they were vigilant in their verbal testimony that, first and foremost, they were servants of a living lord.[12]

It is our contention that this way of seeing things is more relevant to our present situation in missions than we have realized. To illustrate this we will argue that lying behind the New Testament expansion of Christianity was a larger picture that is often obscured in modern readings of Paul's journeys. Our contemporary "model of mission" that calls for moving from the centers of wealth and world power (our *center*) to those who are impoverished physically and spiritually (the *periphery*), has made us blind to the fundamental realities that lay behind the mission of the early church and to the political and economic realities of our own missions structures.

Now it is perfectly natural for us to begin our missionary enterprise where we are, that is, from our own particular Jerusalem, and to move out from there first to neighboring peoples and finally to the ends of the earth. (One might argue that modern missions have mostly overlooked the near neighbors in privileging missions to the periphery; that is another story that we will not rehearse here.) The unique situation of the contemporary missionary movement is that our particular Jerusalem happens to be identified with the absolute centers of political and economic power. Unconsciously we begin to think that there is something natural about missionaries going out from places of power to the "poor souls" in far-flung regions who have little.

In those first days the gospel *did not* go out from a center of power and influence. In fact, the movement pictured in the book of Acts is something of the reverse (one might almost say a parody) of our contemporary missions model, which has taken on all the trappings of the world's greatest centers of power. Uncertain, disorganized and ill-equipped (Galilean!) disciples start out from a distant corner of the Roman Empire. Through various means the gospel spreads through the empire until one of the new recruits, somewhat by accident, ends up (in chains) ministering to believers in Rome! (It is true of course that Paul had in mind a definite urban strategy that certainly included Rome, but his final trip to Rome was not exactly what he had planned—making an interesting parallel, the book of Acts points out, to Jesus' own final trip to Jerusalem!)

Galileans were regarded with virtual contempt in their time. "Can anything good come from Nazareth, the region in which they lived?" snorted the persecutors of Jesus. But this community of "have nots" openly challenged the pinnacles of power in Palestine of their day and conquered them. Contrary to our present-day model, they went from the *periphery* to the *very center* with a triumphant message and earned a hearing by empowerment of the Spirit and sheer boldness.

In contemporary terms a good illustration would be to suppose the gospel would spread from the poorest of poor in Africa to Wall Street in New York, the Miracle Mile in Chicago or the seats of power in Washington, D.C. Perhaps the gospel would capture the hearts of itinerant day laborers in Nigeria and spread by traders throughout Africa. Eventually one of them is assigned to an embassy in Washington, D.C., and starts a small fellowship that acts like an igniting spark. As a matter of fact, this is happening even in our own day—if we could only see beyond the noise and fanfare of our own Western missions publicity promoting *our* exploits among the unreached far from our centers of power!

We catch a glimpse of this exchange between peoples of little significance in Paul's own strategy of missions. While he intended eventually to reach the center of power, Rome, with the gospel, he never envisioned establishing a headquarters there from which all missions activity would radiate. Rather he intended to develop a worldwide network of Christians characterized by love and mutual exchange, to the glory of God. Paul knew that this had theological grounding—that the excellency of the gospel's power rests not in us but in God—and he developed his overall strategy accordingly. Though this strategy has been widely overlooked, it is illustrated in what is known as Paul's collection.[13]

During this period the believers in Jerusalem were experiencing a particularly difficult time of economic hardship. Arguably, a major concern of Paul's third and climactic missionary journey was his systematic collection for these hard-pressed believers living in Jerusalem (see Rom 15:22-33). Perhaps because of an appeal by brothers and sisters in need (Gal 2:10), he undertook a major effort of collecting funds first from the Macedonian churches (who, though they were certainly not rich, were better off than those in Jerusalem) and then from the church at Corinth (2 Cor 8—9).

The issue, Paul explains in 2 Corinthians, was one of fundamental justice, of mutual exchange. The believers in Jerusalem had freely given the good news of Jesus to those in Macedonia and Greece. Now because of recurring famines in Palestine these believers were in a situation of extreme material need. These new believers who had become recipients of the gospel therefore needed to share with their Jerusalem colleagues their material resources.

From the conclusion of the book of Romans, it is clear that Paul understood this to represent the new possibility of a universal sharing between nations represented by the solidarity they now enjoyed in Christ. This solidarity and exchange, he hoped, would make it possible for him to extend the gospel into Spain (Rom 15:22-29).[14] These mutual relationships not only best facilitated the spread of the gospel, Paul believed, but they were themselves an embodiment of that new reality. Jerusalem was only the beginning. Soon Macedonia was playing the sending role, and, eventually, he hoped Rome and Spain would be included in this great work of spreading the rule of Christ.

Back to the Beginning: The Western Heritage of Modern Missions—Millstone or Milestone?
We have come a long way since Jesus' promise of the Spirit and his command to make disciples of all nations. In the first thousand

years, missionaries had reached India and then China. Subsequently Christianity appeared in the Americas and Asia. The last two hundred years in particular appear on the surface to be an amazing fulfillment of that promise. Since William Carey left Britain in 1793, thousands of missionaries from North America and Europe have gone everywhere to take the gospel and plant churches. Today there is a Christian presence in nearly all parts of the world—a fact that is remarkable in and of itself. There is much to be grateful for in all this activity; indeed, during the course of our discussion we will want to highlight some of the genuine advances. If we are to learn from that history, however, we also need to reflect on both its strengths and weaknesses.

For the present we want to call attention to the fact that the modern missionary movement, in its understanding of the center and the periphery, has reflected at every point in its development the Western historical and cultural situation. This fact has led to a model of missions that is often in clear contradiction to Jesus and his early disciples.

There were some undeniable benefits gained from this modern missions strategy, it is true. It cannot be denied that through the prolonged period of Western economic and political dominance, doors were opened worldwide in places that otherwise would have been unreachable. Furthermore, Western prosperity and economic and political stability provided resources as well as opportunity for the extension of the gospel. Analogously, we might argue, the economic and political realities of the Roman Empire provided a unique opportunity for the spread of the gospel in the early church—Paul was able to use his Roman citizenship to good effect on more than one occasion.

But there is a dark side to this modern story as well. The political and economic relationships between the West and non-West not infrequently resulted in oppressive structures that impeded the real development of these places. Sadly, the effects (even the reality) of these structures often persist to this day. In the illuminating phrase of Jonathan Bonk, missionaries were often allied with colonialism even if they were "reluctant imperialists."[15]

Nevertheless missionaries were inevitably linked with this period of Western dominance, and when they spoke of their Jerusalem, it was always the seat of the political and economic power of the modern world. As Lamin Sanneh observed, "Mission acquired the status of western religious mischief in the wider context of European and American Imperialism."[16]

We acknowledge that much has changed in recent years. But Orlando Costas's assessment of thirty years ago remains true in many respects: "As far back as William Carey and as recently as the Lausanne movement the financial backbone of a lot of the churches and missionary societies that we represent is to be found among those who possessed wealth, knowledge, and power, indeed among those who control."[17] There are parts of the world—one thinks for example of China—where the failure of the missionary enterprise is clearly linked to its identification with Western power and influence. This part of missions history has yet to be written.

But missionaries not only reflected their political situation, they also carried their cultural values with them as well. Unfortunately, there was a widespread assumption, even if unarticulated, that the culture of the missionary was far superior to anything encountered elsewhere. For example, missionaries in the early nineteenth century were able to raise funds and go abroad because they came together and formed themselves into voluntary societies. Now we have come to take for granted the role of such free associations, but in important ways they represent particular cultural assumptions and a specific historical situation. The ability to form associations of this kind assumed the freedom of individuals to come together around a common task, but it also depended on the view that religion was primarily a private and spiritual affair that only indirectly affects society.[18]

While one might debate whether this worldview was good or bad or how biblical it was, it is indisputable that these values were not shared in cultures to which missionaries were sent. Inevitably missionary attitudes and practices and the structures that resulted were shaped in ways that reflected their Western values and contradicted, often in tragic ways, the cultural realities of the host countries. Fortunately, the missiology of today has changed radically in this respect compared with the past, and missionaries are apt to be highly trained in anthropology. But too often the programs and structures continue to reflect cultural values that conflict with the message we are ostensibly bringing—or even with our own newly minted cultural sensitivities! Contemporary missions retain, one might say, a kind of structural hangover that continues to impede a genuine openness to the work of God.

What this means, using the analogy of the times in which Jesus lived, is that Rome (i.e., a Western country) was the missionaries' home and center politically, culturally and even economically. Jerusalem, Judea and Galilee, then, would have been seen as part of the periphery and a tempting target for missions activity because they represented such great need and were so impoverished. All of this of course is the reverse of the biblical pattern.

Western missionaries may not have consciously thought in these terms. But it is undeniable that the countries on the periphery were seen as both inferior and filled with heathen peoples without the gospel. As was quite natural the missionaries of that time would take with them all the education, resources and techniques that they thought they might need and then travel—preferably over a large body of water—to some distant place where missions activities would be carried out.

Although much good was accomplished and the gospel was advanced—and indeed missionaries personally often sacrificed a great deal in leaving home, this gospel message was invariably associated with the political, economic and cultural power that these missionaries represented. Moreover, what is even more significant for our discussion, this association was often unconsciously reflected in its accompanying enterprises—sending organizations, training institutions, media and the like.

Ironically, most who are missionaries today no longer carry the attitudes of those who founded these institutions. But the structural reality of Mission, Inc., a vast enterprise, often speaks louder than the well-intended pronouncements of its leaders. This tension represents one of the greatest challenges for the future. It is illustrated in the struggle that Global Harvest Mission and many others like it are currently undergoing.

Facing a Future That Is Not Linked to Western History

Whatever the success of the modern missionary movement to date, it faces a future that is totally unlike the period during which it achieved these successes. Ever since the end of World War II, and definitively since the fall of the Berlin Wall, prevailing concepts of what represents the *center* and what represents the *periphery* have radically changed in political, cultural and economic terms. The reality is that nearly all countries or people groups formerly designated as lying at the periphery no longer take their political cues from the West (or the North).

Culturally it no longer makes any sense to speak of Western culture, or even North American culture in any unified sense, for we are faced with a cultural pluralism that defies the framework of center and periphery. Economically, North Americans are likely to be driving a Japanese car, wearing a shirt made in Taiwan, eating fruit imported from South America or Israel and investing in mutual funds that profit from activities in China and India.

Some countries previously associated with the periphery are now economic powerhouses in their own right; others, tragically, are relatively poorer than when our missionary forebears first traveled there a hundred years ago. In all of these instances talk of a center and a periphery is no longer appropriate and often misleading. While the modern development of missions was associated with centers of power and influence, today those places where economic power resides are *not* important centers of Christianity, and the most vital Christian communities are found in areas of limited political and economic power.[19] What this means, in no uncertain terms, is that *past practices cannot continue to be the model for the future of missions.*

Our dilemma then can be put in these terms: *while our mission structures and attitudes have been formed by a particular historical and cultural situation, missions must now be carried out in a wholly different situation.* Here is where our reflection in this chapter on Jesus' instructions and the practice of the early church takes on renewed importance.

A new missionary situation. Given the radical upheaval in what now is considered to be center versus periphery, missionary activity has become radically decentralized. Jerusalems are springing up everywhere! In fact, the most important "centers" are mostly invisible (and often simply inaccessible) to Western observers. As we will argue in the next chapter, the better model for conceiving of missions, consistent with the emerging postmodern consciousness, is multiple centers of influence making up a network of mutual exchange and support. A few illustrations provide a sense of the present situation.

One of the most interesting missions initiatives is a growing movement of African missions to North America. A group of churches formed by the Nigerian-based Deeper Life Bible Fellowship has planted congregations across America. Furthermore, Action Chapel, a Ghanaian denomination, has established an outreach in the nation's capital and even holds regular Bible studies in the World Bank offices in Washington. This African style of worship is attracting many non-Africans because it is so alive and joyful.

One pastor with the Nigerian-based Redeemed Christian Church of God in Tallahassee explains the popularity of these churches by noting that "the church in Africa is on fire, while the church in America is, for the most part, losing its zeal."[20] These missionaries face many obstacles, but their zeal and vitality reflect the growth of their home churches, which now boast more than 20 percent of the world's Christians.

In September 1997 a second Asian Missions Congress met in Pattaya, Thailand, and drew 388 participants from twenty-one nations in Asia. This group, with thoroughly Asian leadership, represented missions that did not exist a generation ago but are now taking the lead in reaching out to peoples throughout this vast continent. They represent countries like Japan and Korea with vast economic resources, as well as places like Vietnam and Thailand with a vigorous church but few resources. Together they are partnering in various ways to extend the kingdom, reaching places totally inaccessible to Western missionaries. Most interesting is the fact that gatherings of this kind are as common as they are invisible to Western Christians.[21]

Stories like these could be multiplied—Chinese missionaries in Cambodia, Korean missionaries in Africa and Russia, Filipino missionaries in Latin America, the Middle East, and so on. But all of this illustrates that the most vital centers of missions—the Jerusalems of today—are now dispersed throughout the world. Lamin Sanneh argues in fact that "Christianity triumphs by the relinquishing of Jerusalem or any fixed center."[22]

A time for radical change. The changed world situation that we have described suggests a new metaphor for understanding missions. It is no longer appropriate to send missionaries and even resources from a dominant center of political or economic influence to some distant and exotic place. Indeed world structures have come to reflect much more a network of relationships that defy a fixed sense of place. This has led some people to speak of the "end of geography." In economics for example, Paul Hawken points out, "Global financial integration, fed by information and communication technologies, has rendered the very concept of place irrelevant."[23] As a result, a better metaphor for the present situation in missions is a network—conceived as *mutual exchange between multiple centers of missionary influence.*

As Andrew Walls puts it:

> The territorial "from-to" idea that underlay the older missionary movement has to give way to a concept much more like that of Christians within the Roman Empire in the second and third centuries: parallel presence in different circles and at different levels each seeking to penetrate within and beyond its circle.[24]

When one looks closely at the modern movement in missions, this kind of serendipity and Christian exchange from diverse parts of the world is not an unusual phenomenon. A wonderful example is the 1907 Azusa Street Mission in Los Angeles. After studying with Charles Parham, one of the founders of the Pentecostal movement, African-American holiness preacher William Seymour came to Los

Angeles in 1906 to begin his ministry—which at that time was hardly a center of power. When he was dismissed from his pastorate because he advocated speaking in tongues, he began meeting with a small band of believers in a home on North Bonnie Brae Street.

Soon the crowds forced them to move to a dilapidated building on Azusa Street where thousands of people began coming to the three daily meetings. Many of these came from overseas and took the revival and ministry of the Holy Spirit with them to their home countries. Frank Bartleman was so touched by the Pentecostal message that he was motivated to spread it across this country as well as overseas. Gaston Cashwell came from North Carolina, experienced the touch of God, and returned home to become the "Pentecostal Apostle to the South." C. H. Mason came from Jackson, Mississippi, and experienced the gift of the Spirit and returned to Memphis, Tennessee, to found the Church of God in Christ, which is today the largest African-American denomination in the United States.[25]

It is remarkable that men, women, black, white, all came together to experience their modern-day "pentecost" and returned with their newfound treasure in what became the start of the modern pentecostal movement. With minimal education and little social standing, often the object of public mockery and scorn, these people were nevertheless used by God to extend the kingdom in ways that recall the book of Acts. Unfortunately, it is also true that their subsequent histories are not without the same tensions and divisions that the New Testament recounts.

Such illustrations could be multiplied. They point to the fact that partnership and exchange, openness to the Spirit's leading, and sheer providential intervention have been at the heart of some of the most important advances in missions since the time of the New Testament. But equally important is the fact that we find ourselves in a particular cultural situation in which the technological and political realities favor informal and ad hoc strategies that meet particular and often quite temporary needs. The problem we must contend with is that Mission, Inc., has developed a sophisticated missions apparatus with complex lines of communications, patterns of fundraising and multiple layers of administration. While all of this can be quite impressive and has been important in the past, at present it does not facilitate mutual exchange between parts of the body of Christ or encourage spontaneity. The plot line we ought to seek is not the history of our mission, certainly not that of the imperial West, but that of the reign of God as it extends itself throughout, back and forth, and across the world.

As Orlando Costas put it in the 1970s, the crisis of contemporary missions results from the "one-way street mentality."[26] In other words, structures have been developed to facilitate the flow of personnel and resources from the center to the periphery. In his opinion the only solution is a willingness to undertake a radical restructuring that enables and facilitates the two-way traffic appropriate to the new situation in missions. Almost a century ago Roland Allen argued that our missionary methods had departed in important ways from those of the apostle Paul. Our sense of a people's lack of development, he argued, has led to oppressive missionary structures. He concluded, "Our difficulty is that we have not yet tried St. Paul's method anywhere, and have used the same argument to bolster up our dread of independence everywhere."[27]

At the end of our century the missionary establishment in the West is beginning to recognize this challenge and is struggling to respond. But the results to date are meager. A Sri Lankan missiologist, Vinoth Ramachandra, puts it well: "A partnership that involves thoughtful, mutual listening among Christians from every tradition and culture within the world wide Church is indispensable for faithful united witness to Jesus Christ."[28] Sadly, Ramachandra concludes, today the possibilities for this much needed mutuality appear bleak.

Can the Shackles Be Broken?

No one on the missions committee at the First Church of Rollingwood could have conceived what God was going to show them as they reviewed the Gospels and the book of Acts. They entered into this along with James Morey from the Global Harvest Mission with open hearts and minds. And God met them in some very exciting ways.

From the very outset of their study, they quickly grasped that

God indeed is a missionary God. They found themselves captivated by the story that unfolded as the disciples and other followers of Jesus began to grasp just what this meant.

☐ A small group from Galilee, an area largely despised and disregarded, dared to move from the political, social and economic periphery to challenge the very centers of power in the Roman world as they followed their Lord and Master.

☐ The message they brought was radically and distinctly countercultural, one that would strike to the very heart of what had gone wrong among the very people that God himself chose to be his ambassadors to the entire world. No one could escape a burning searchlight that revealed the total barrenness of self-seeking and worldly power.

☐ They came as a band of disciples, a committed community calling itself a church, who literally "turned the world upside down," ordinary people empowered to live under the lordship of their King and Savior while committed to righteousness and justice.

☐ The beliefs they practiced laid bare a religion that indeed had become twenty miles wide and one inch deep—outwardly godly, inwardly barren and corrupt. And it launched a quiet revolution that has continued for two thousand years, in spite of the ebbs and flows of indifference and diminished vitality within the very church itself.

☐ These disciples took their King at his word when he told them to join with him in his mission to go and make disciples everywhere. They were keenly aware that this only could take place when their godly and radically different lives, motivated by divine love, prompted others to ask for the reason, for the hope that was within them.

☐ Without fear they testified to a living Lord who reigns today, who opens his kingdom to all who will die to self and emerge as a new creature. Only a minority responded, as always is the case, but this "company of the committed" set in motion a worldwide transformation that continues to this day.

One of the members of this study group, Sandy Gallagher,

said it best when she commented, "I have always heard that God has put his church on earth only to announce the good news and do everything possible to win others to Christ. All my life I have felt like little more than a salesperson for Jesus. Most of the time I just shut up and try to live the best life I can on the job by being ethical and concerned for others. And I have felt like such a failure because I am not a soul winner like some of the others in the church." Others voiced the same sentiments.

Pastor Geoff Finch got right to the issue with this thoughtful comment. "I now see that we are not supposed to 'win' the world through evangelism. All God wants us to do is to be a faithful community of believers committed to be an alternative to an unjust materialistic world sold out to self-seeking. As we do this in our daily lives and share the hope, we are going to make a real difference that others will notice and be attracted to." Geoff went on to say that the sagging world missions program at First Church is just a symptom of an inward focus on self-fulfillment and satisfaction that is a far cry from all that Jesus said in the Gospels about his expectations of his church. He summed it up by saying, "We really aren't all that different from the world itself. It's time to rediscover Christ's 'narrow way.'"

James Morey from GHM had been silent during these deliberations, primarily because of the growing discomfort he felt over the sagging vitality in the mission. Finally he too spoke out, and his words struck home. "We have turned the Great Commission into a great commotion of words and more words as we have tried to make converts on the field. We have planted many churches, but we have not made disciples committed to the values of the kingdom of Christ. And what do we have to show for it? Large numbers in some places but not much more. It's time for some radical rethinking."

*   *   *

In short, both First Church and GHM took the first small steps toward a process of restoration and renewal that would have dramatic future consequences. Our readers will find implications leaping to mind as they contemplate how missions theology and practice must change. But we ask you to stay with us on this journey. For we will soon see why much of our current practice will prove increasingly counterproductive unless changes are forthcoming quickly.

In chapter three we will further unpack the complex of issues that will help us understand how missions fell into captivity to Western culture. We will discover that our current practice to a great degree is far more reflective of the America of the late 1800s and early 1900s than it is either of biblical patterns or today's dynamics. We will call for an end to reliance on outmoded paradigms and for a return to what Jesus taught and exemplified. Once this basis is in place, we will move directly into the steps necessary to revitalize our far-flung but sagging Western missionary enterprise.

The implications for both local churches and mission agencies will be far-reaching and, in some cases, even traumatic. But a continued reliance on the shaky and often erroneous theological and strategic foundations of Western missions will all but erode the impact of a once vital Christian presence in the world.

3

....

What's Gone Wrong
with the Harvest?

The small group that launched this eye-opening study of the biblical perspective on world missions quickly began to grow. Soon others from the senior staff team of Global Harvest Mission (GHM) joined along with some genuine seekers from First Church. It wasn't long before a short evening meeting expanded to a full Saturday morning each week.

Few will ever forget that Saturday when Bud Anderson, president of GHM, attended for the first time and shared what God was saying to him. He began with the frank admission that GHM and many other agencies have almost lost sight of the biblical principles that are emerging in fresh new ways through this group. James Morey had faithfully shared these each week in GHM staff meetings, and few had been left untouched.

Bud had been especially disturbed by the extent to which we seem to have lost track of what Jesus said about the kingdom of God. He opened the book of Matthew and shared his insights.

"God's reign in his kingdom, like the mustard seed, starts almost invisibly but becomes a tree of such dimensions that birds of the air will come and perch in its branches (Mt 13:32). It now is clear to me that Jesus was referring to how his church demonstrates his reign in the world. It must be a 'company of the committed' living under the lordship of Christ who will bear the very fruit of Jesus, who was 'anointed . . . to preach the good news to the poor . . . to proclaim freedom for the prisoners and recovery of sight for the blind, to release the oppressed, to proclaim the year of the Lord's favor'" (Lk 4:18-19).

Bud went on to ask, "Why is it, then, that so many sectors of the historically Christian parts of the world and other areas experiencing rapid church growth still are caught so deeply in the grip of unrestrained materialism and increasing concentration of wealth in the hands of a few? Why are crushing burdens of oppression on those who are weak and powerless tolerated and even ignored? Why are moral values and public behavior, even in areas with substantial Christian presence, deteriorating to depths not even seen in Sodom and Gomorrah? Surely these are not the fruits that are expected from those who are Jesus' disciples."

Bud concluded with this sobering observation. "I can only conclude that most of us who are committed to world missions have seriously lost our way. The church of Jesus Christ and a bunch of agencies like GHM have become like a tree with a meager yield of fruit. We are just kidding ourselves by all this propaganda that the Great Commission is almost fulfilled. Our theology and our methods have become nearly bankrupt."

These were strong words, and several pointed out that there are a number of exceptions, especially in those parts of the world where the church has regained vitality. But there was agreement all around the room that something indeed has gone wrong with the harvest as the church enters a new millennium.

*   *   *

IT IS OUR CONTENTION THAT THIS INCREASINGLY MEAGER HARVEST of kingdom righteousness reflects a Westernized theology and practice of world missions that has deviated from its historic biblical roots. In this chapter we explore what has happened to bring about this change in outlook and behavior within the church in Western countries as well as other parts of the world.

We will discover three ways in which Western Christians over the last two centuries have been influenced by the spirit of the age:

1. by their two crucial omissions from the Great Commission

2. by their reducing of world missions to a managerial enterprise

3. by their displacing the local church from its rightful place at the center of world outreach

Three Competing Worldviews

Religious expression in any country or society is inescapably influenced by the prevailing worldview—the lens of values and beliefs through which reality is viewed. This is, of course, inevitable, and there is no question that the continuing translation of the gospel can open up new and exciting perspectives on biblical truth. But there are dangers as well, which we do well to acknowledge. Our focus here primarily is on America because of the unique role this country has played in shaping current missionary strategy worldwide, although Great Britain and Europe were similarly affected.

Bob Fryling has proposed a vivid way to clarify primary worldviews since the dawn of Christianity.[1] Picture if you will three very different individuals, each of whom represents a radically different outlook and way of thinking:

1. a robed priest in medieval times bound by belief in divine authority, revealed truth, absolute rules and accepted rituals

2. a scientist in her white coat, intent on her electronic microscope, boldly confident that modern science and culture will reveal truth through reason and rationality

3. a bearded, scruffy-looking rock musician disillusioned with both traditional and modern culture, seeking to make meaning out of a life that is futile and disillusioning

The priest represents the *traditional theocentric* worldview of the church from shortly after the time of Christ through the Enlightenment. The source of all truth and path to all knowledge is divine revelation. This is clearly captured by the words of Augustine, who said, "*I believe in order that I might know.*" Even more to the point is Anselm's *credo ut intelligem*—"*I believe in order that I might understand.*" All human reasoning, then, is subject to validation against Scripture. Today this outlook lives on virtually unchanged in some sectors of the church, most notably in the Catholic and Orthodox traditions.

The white-coated scientist, on the other hand, represents *modernity*, a worldview skeptical of traditionalism and its rules and superstitions. She is the symbol of a worldview that places bold confidence in the empirical search for truth. The new standard of truth is the scientific method, often felt to be incompatible with traditional authority.

The rock musician, the last of the three, is a fairly recent entry on a montage of competing worldviews and is anything but confident in either traditionalism with its narrowed latitudes, or modernity with its emphasis on rationality and progress. This person is *postmodern*, questioning the ability of anyone to know and understand. His or her world, after all, has been one where human "wisdom" and technology have led to Auschwitz, nuclear war, Kosovo, East Timor and environmental degradation. Interestingly, in spite of deep disillusionment, postmoderns have rescued from the refuse heap of history the value of the person, experience and faith. In short, postmodernism, at least in its relatively early stages, represents a pendulum swing that McLaren and others[2] view as one of the greatest opportunities of history for the Christian faith.

The Displacement of Traditionalism by Modernity

Of these three worldviews, modernity—the contemporary liberated secular society—is still dominant for most people, and it is sweeping the world through such carriers as market capitalism, political revolution, industrial technology, burgeoning population growth, mass media and urbanization.[3] It had its birth during and after the renaissance, when a newly revived Greek rationality and an ambitious exploration of the world produced modern science with its focus on empirical reasoning.[4] This led to a titanic struggle within the church over faith and rationality.

An early probable factor in what was to be a crumbling of the supremacy of divine revelation was the attempt by medieval theologian Thomas Aquinas to distinguish between two kinds of knowledge: truth that could be known by unaided reason over and against that which originates only from God and his revelation. This split tempted later thinkers to attempt to show that Christianity can be defended at the bar of reason without challenging the often unnoticed assumption that human wisdom can discern ultimate truth.[5]

The way was now open wide to developments that would in later centuries relegate Christian faith to the realm of unverifiable values that an individual is free to accept or reject. The ultimate outcome was a fundamental tenet of the *great Enlightenment* that the only *reliable knowledge* is that which has achieved mathematical clarity and *objectivity* through reason guided by scientific method. Anything outside of these boundaries, including religious faith, is to be regarded as *subjective* and open to doubt.

Once this duality of knowledge and truth became accepted, we entered the age of *modernity*, in which Augustine's basic tenet became corrupted and restated as "*I know, therefore I am.*" Human reason and individualism now reigned supreme as the dominant spirit of the age. The quantum leaps in technology, especially in the last two hundred years, fueled a great optimism that the world can be changed and conquered. The cry of Western civilization and the very essence of modernity became "*There is no problem too big that it cannot be solved with human wisdom and technology!*"

A fundamental premise of modernity is that each individual is assumed to have the capacity to grasp the realities of nature and morality.[6] Divine revelation, since it appears to deal primarily in the realm of belief and values, is relegated to the private world and is not allowed to make claims about public life. In other words, religion deals with *meaning*, whereas science reveals *truth*. Ultimately, values and meanings simply become a matter of personal choice. In this intellectual environment the claim of Jesus that "I am the way, the truth and the life" cannot have any universal validity. The outcome, of course, is an insidious and ultimately devastating undermining of the very foundations of traditional Christianity.

A crucial schism was created, therefore, that continues to influence Western thought and action. It takes this form:

Private (*supernatural, sacred, values, private*): theology, religion, ethics

contrasted with

Public (*natural, secular, facts, public*): physical sciences, social sciences, economics, management, education and politics[7]

Christianity and all other religions are relegated to the private sector and banished, in effect, from the public sector and from daily life in general. Even more important, all things are subject to doubt and scrutiny; yet only scientifically derived fact is considered to be *objective* and true. Religious values are believed to represent matters of opinion, personal preference or subjective choice rather than objective, public truth. The unfortunate outcome is the widespread view that religion is ultimately irrelevant and will finally be replaced by reason in a secular society. It was this assumption that led in our century to the rise of highly centralized organizations like the United Nations and later the International Monetary Fund and the World Bank, which would be the means for applying reason and good sense to the problems of the world.

To recapitulate, here are the main outcomes of modernity:

☐ The emancipation of the human mind from the confines of traditionalism and its presupposition that divine revelation is the standard for all truth.

☐ The elevation of individualism as the guiding force for progress.

☐ A pervasive belief that science is neutral, value free and factual. Everything else falls into the category of subjective, unprovable values that must, of necessity, be a matter of personal belief confined to one's private world—religion thus was irrelevant to the major issues of life.

☐ A secularism that assumes that all societies will evolve to the point that reason would ultimately rule as supreme, leading to the development of huge, highly centralized institutions that embody this faith in the triumph of reason.

☐ An optimistic conviction that all problems are solvable through the combination of individual initiative, reasoning and technology.

The Invasion of Modernity into Christianity

The modern missions movement as we know it was born during the Enlightenment in the eighteenth century. And it must be recognized that the entry of modernity, at the outset, was liberating for humankind and the church. Indeed it emancipated humanity from a sense of hopelessness and passivity. It is crucially important to grasp this point because it illustrates that all cultural movements are ambiguous. Modernity, which was a positive and liberating influence in some ways, also proved to be dangerous to the health of the church.

Yes, positive, fresh winds of change swept through the church. Christians discovered anew that Spirit-empowered reflection, reasoning and action can bring about changes surpassing their greatest dreams. Futility and hopelessness gave way to optimism and creativity and thereby restored the realities of hope that the gospel always has been able to infuse into static and traditional culture. During this time, special impetus was provided by the great awakenings that swept across both Great Britain and the United States in the late eighteenth century. Christians were encouraged to embrace their faith with genuine vigor as the means to reform their world and usher in a new age characterized by justice and prosperity.

Religious revival at that time was characterized by the balanced and holistic conception of the reign of God discussed in chapter two. It manifested genuine piety and rigorous commitment to abolishment of grievous social abuses. The United States proved to be an especially fertile seedbed because of its Puritan heritage. In the words of Mark Noll:

> The distinguishing characteristic of Puritanism was its effort to unite the theology of the Reformation with a comprehensive view of the world. . . . Puritans were convinced that a vital personal religion was the wellspring of all earthly good. They were equally convinced that all aspects of life—whether political, social, cultural, economic, artistic, or ecclesiastical—needed to be brought into subjection to God.[8]

The most visible manifestation of a kingdom-based Christianity was a Christ-centered morality literally penetrating all sectors of life. As a result of nineteenth century revivals, sanctification and holiness emerged as the pervasive focus across the church. Domestic violence, drunkenness, prostitution and open disregard of social morality and the law abated significantly.[9] Revival, in turn, led to sweeping social transformation that took such forms as generosity toward the poor, an end to black slave trade and slavery in England and later in the United States, reforms for white laborers, prison reform, relief and rescue missions, orphanages, universal education and radical reform of oppressive legal structures.[10]

As a part of this same impetus, world missions was rescued from many centuries of virtual neglect. The modern missionary movement owes a great debt to William Carey, who was among the first to catch the attention of Christians in 1792 when he published a pamphlet exegeting Matthew 28:18-20 entitled *An Inquiry into the Obligations of Christians to Use Means for the Conversion of the Heathen.* Throughout his lifetime Carey captured the spirit of the times with his exhortation "Expect great things from God, attempt great things for God."

Since William Carey left Great Britain in 1793, thousands of missionaries from Europe and North America have taken the gospel and planted churches in all parts of the world. Today there is a Christian presence in most countries of the world. But, as we have noted, if we are to build on that history, we also need to reflect on both the strengths and weaknesses of this missions advance.

Carey initiated a missionary cause that was soon fueled by a pervasive optimism that Christianity could, if proclaimed properly, reform an entire world and bring about a millennial golden age. In fact, world missions was embraced in the United States in particular as a kind of manifest national destiny.[11]

These early missions efforts reflected the very essence of the Puritan heritage through a healthy focus on the mission statement of Jesus himself as revealed in Luke 4. Indeed these were exhilarating times, reflecting a postmillennial expectation that the reign of Christ could become a tangible, earthly reality. This optimism, however, was challenged by the devastation of the Civil War in the 1860s as well as World War I, when the cancerous effects of unbridled modernity were to become apparent within Protestant ranks. There were three ways in which this took place: (1) two facets were omitted from the Great Commission, (2) world missions was reduced to a managerial enterprise, (3) the local church was institutionally displaced from the center of world outreach.

Two Omissions from the Great Commission

In the early decades of the twentieth century the American church tended toward two distinctly opposite poles. One branch (soon to be labeled as liberal) refused to abdicate its optimistic commitment to social transformation as the central mission of the church. Unfortunately, the salvation of souls diminished in priority, thus giving way to what was known as the *social gospel*. The other branch (the fundamentalists) responded in opposite fashion by stressing "the dangers of the world, the comforts of a separated piety, the centrality of evangelism, and an expectation of the end."[12]

As a result, basic Christian truths were increasingly maintained by evangelicals by fleeing from the problems of the world into fascination with inner spiritual life and the details of end times prophecy. These developments, themselves an indirect product of the modern worldview, were a primary source of a specious dichotomy between evangelism (spiritual) and social transformation (physical), which continues to destroy much of the essence of the message of the church in today's world.

This conservative Christian aversion to social action served to distort the holistic biblical worldview in which God has created all things to reflect his glory. Indeed the very essence of God's redemptive work is "to reconcile to himself all things, whether things on earth or things in heaven, by making peace through his blood, shared on the cross" (Col 1:20). From creation to the new heaven and earth, God seeks to redeem and integrate the physical and spiritual, rather than to separate them.

Needless to say, the world mission of the church of God as it interpreted the call of Matthew 28:18-20 was splintered and dismembered. This privatistic retreat was manifested in two particularly unfortunate ways: (1) a dichotomy between evangelism and social transformation, and (2) evangelism void of discipleship.

A dichotomy between evangelism and social transformation. All of us who have lived through the ongoing social carnage of the twentieth century can appreciate the crisis of shattered postmillennial optimism among evangelicals after the Civil War and the awful world wars of this century. Battles were fought with unprecedented losses and the dismemberment of an entire way of life. It is not surprising that most would turn in an entirely opposite direction and abandon the seemingly futile cause of social reform.

Who can fault legendary evangelist Dwight L. Moody, who captured the mood of evangelicals at the end of the nineteenth century, in his declaration, *"I look upon the world as a wrecked vessel. God has given me a lifeboat and said to me, 'Moody, save all you can.'"*[13] In other words, all hopes of transforming society with the gospel were dashed, in his eyes, until Christ's return in glory, leaving only one option, *the lifeboat*—a single-minded focus on evangelism as the mission of the church.

While few would echo the words of Moody and his contemporaries today, we still hear a distinct but largely unrecognized carryover. Ever since the late 1800s, dominant evangelical voices have called for accelerated church planting to *evangelize the maximum number of unreached in the shortest possible period of time.* The return of Christ became the dominant motivation for missions—only this return would bring about the transformation that the gospel required. The only human effort required was an announcement of the message. Quite understandably Matthew 24:14 became the premier guiding text for missions with its assurance that the end will come once the gospel of the kingdom is "preached in the whole world as a testimony to all nations."

There never has been a dispute that evangelism is indispensable as the first step in making disciples in all nations, but now voices were heard calling for the first time for completion of world evangelization in this generation. It would almost seem as if the future of the world and the ultimate victory of Christ had become dependent upon human initiative. Little wonder that evangelicals were quick to embrace the wonders of a technological age and to mobilize Christian resources in an unprecedented way. In the process it became tempting to disregard the essence of the Great Commission traced in chapter two, where it is abundantly obvious that human efforts are futile, or at least inadequate, without the convicting, regenerating and sanctifying role of the Holy Spirit.

Furthermore, among those who referred to themselves as *evangelicals*, there was almost total silence in response to God's call for social justice to alleviate the burdens of ignorance, poverty and hunger, racism, the loss of cultural identity, and other forms of oppression (Amos 5:21-24; Lk 3:10-14; 4:18-21). Os Guinness prophetically observed that the outcome of this silence is *a church that has lost its impact by becoming "privately engaging, socially irrelevant."*[14]

Guinness uses the analogy of the Cheshire Cat in the famous story *Alice in Wonderland* by Lewis Carroll. In this fable, the cat gradually loses its identity until all that remains is its famous lingering grin. So it is with the church, which by and large now has only the "lingering grin," a surface indicator of a privatized faith without moral and social impact. In so doing, the church has dug its own grave, while the smile lingers on.

What a contrast this "lingering grin" is to John Wesley's vision of the church as "a body . . . compacted together, in order, first, to save each his [sic] own soul; then to assist each other in working out salvation; and afterwards, as far as in them lies, to save all from present and future misery, to overturn the kingdom of Satan, and to set up the kingdom of Christ."[15] Wesley and his esteemed colleague George Whitefield clearly demonstrated in eighteenth-century England and the United States that a profound and lasting impact is made on society through evangelism coupled with sweeping social transformation, not by evangelism alone.

We must challenge the validity of evangelism without social transformation, however, from yet another perspective. What, after all, is the message? Is it simply a restatement of some particular biblical information that we call the plan of salvation? If so, this grossly violates the model provided by Jesus and the apostles. As a rule, acts of healing, power or compassion were *followed by* preaching given in response to the question "What is this new reality?" As Newbigin points out, this question is only asked if there is some evidence that a new reality is present.[16] That reality is Jesus and the impact of his life on his followers. This was the new reality embodied in the message carried by believers who were described as "those who have turned the world upside down." This was their "message."

We seem to have reversed the order by preaching the good news first, followed by formation of a church, which, it is hoped, will demonstrate compassion and holy living. Tragically, it would appear that we have the cart before the horse. Unfortunately our message becomes barren of substance where there is little tangible behavior to substantiate our claims.

Evangelism void of discipleship. It also is common practice among Western evangelicals to declare that the Great Commission will be *fulfilled* when each person has had opportunity to be exposed to the gospel through evangelistic initiatives. But we must ask, whatever happened to the command to make disciples? Dallas Willard is precisely right when he prophetically observes that the evangelical church is guilty of making *converts* and not *disciples.* In so doing it perpetuates *a great omission in the Great Commission.*[17]

His reference, of course, is to evangelism largely devoid of intentional spiritual formation that "prepare[s] God's people for works of service" (Eph 4:12) over and beyond Sunday morning proclamation and teaching. In his words, "The doctrinal struggles of many centuries . . . transformed saving faith into *mere mental assent* to correct doctrine."[18] This is a serious capitulation to the spirit of modernity that confines faith only to the private world of self-actualization and meaning or to the acceptance of some propositional truth. As a result, the entire public sector in most places is all-too-frequently devoid of Christians who witness by following their master in modeling justice, righteousness and peace.

When the Great Commission is properly conceived as making disciples, it should then become apparent that disciple-making is a process that will continue until Christ returns. In other words, the

Great Commission can *never be fulfilled,* and we are doing a great disservice when we declare any part of the world to have been *reached.*

The Reduction of World Missions to a Managerial Enterprise
According to an oft-repeated dictum of Martin Luther, the Lion of Judah does not need us to defend him, he just needs to be released. Most evangelicals believe this is true of the gospel, but those with North American addresses sometimes act as if the Lion could use help. As a result, North American missions has become known for technical and organizational brilliance and highly centralized bureaucratic structures. Indeed one might say that one of the greatest strengths of North American missions, and, we will argue, one of its greatest weaknesses, is its preoccupation with strategies and methods.[19]

American evangelicals, for at least the last two hundred years, have been known for their use of the most up-to-date methods in evangelism and missions. Since the time of Charles Finney and the frontier growth of the "Methodists" (so-called because of their strict use of methods in ordering and developing the Christian life), evangelicals have been quick to adopt modern techniques. Camp meetings took advantage of the frontier situation; mass evangelism later in the century adapted itself to its urban setting.

As soon as the radio came into common use, evangelists took advantage of this means to reach out to people with the gospel. Later, television and now even the Internet have become privileged means of spreading the gospel. Today so-called seeker-sensitive churches use contemporary music and state-of-the-art technology to attract people.

Much of this, of course, may represent a prudent following of Paul's counsel to become all things to all people so that, by any means, we can save some (1 Cor 9:22). Furthermore, Scripture is full of admonitions and instruction on organizational stewardship. Certainly one cannot deny that the world of technology and managerial skill has rich resources to mine. But at the core of this adaptation of American pragmatism is a disturbing irony—while evangelicals have been quick to discern and denounce theological modernism, they have been all too willing to embrace sociological modernism uncritically.[20] As a result, their use of contemporary technology is often open to challenges.

Certainly this focus is a major reason for the present crisis in missions. Strategies and plans for world evangelization have multiplied to such an extent that a recent evaluation of American missions arrived at the conclusion that we have become victims of our communication strategies.[21] John Seel puts this problem as bluntly as possible: "The American Evangelical movement is deeply infiltrated by the spirit and tools of modernity. Oblivious to its dangers, American evangelicalism continues as one of the leading global apologists for modernity through its publications and mission agencies."[22] This is a strong charge to make, but as the following pages reveal, we feel it has merit.

It also is an undeniable fact that Western agencies have assumed a dominant world position, an issue that was discussed at length in the preceding chapter. From one point of view, this is a profound sign that God's call to world missions was taken seriously for many decades and responded to on a scale unmatched in world history. But at the same time, we cannot overlook the obvious fact that the vast economic and technological resources that were mobilized and deployed worldwide had enormous consequences for the practice of missions.

There are three resulting problems that contribute to the current malaise in missions. On the one hand, a preoccupation with methods and numbers has often obscured larger questions of the ultimate goal of missions. Indeed we will argue that our methods have tended to undermine those goals. But, equally seriously, our method-driven missions in many cases have had the following unintended consequences: (1) an uncritical adoption of strategic planning, (2) a preoccupation with numerical success, and (3) an unhealthy relationship between numerical success and funding.

Uncritical adoption of strategic planning. The modern missions movement, of course, experienced its birth at the zenith of the Enlightenment. And it is a deeply ingrained cultural value for Americans that any problem carefully analyzed and understood can be appropriately addressed and (usually) solved.[23] Furthermore, an abundance of human and natural resources, especially in North America, has fueled a pervasive optimism that any venture, no matter its size or complexity, will thrive and grow.

It was not long before evangelism, now the primary preoccupation of the conservative church, was defined as *the act of presenting the plan of salvation*. In other words, the gospel was summarized in the form of its basic propositions—God's love, the human sin nature, Christ's sacrifice, and the need for a tangible response of accepting Christ. Once this step was taken, the pragmatism so evident as a product of the Enlightenment gave rise to a hunger for strategies that would produce results within a given time period. Such great evangelists as Finney and Moody, for example, openly embraced and discarded strategies on the basis of the numbers of resulting converts, a practice commonplace today.

While this quest for greater Christian stewardship is laudable, it quickly can lead to the seductive temptation to reduce world missions to a manageable enterprise—with a large hierarchical structure to carry it out. Samuel Escobar has coined the phrase "managerial missiology" to refer to an unduly pragmatic endeavor "to reduce reality to an understandable picture, and then to project missionary action as a response to a problem that has been described in quantitative form."[24]

Once evangelism has been conceptualized into presentation of propositional truth, it is a logical deduction to declare a person (or even a people group) as "reached" or "evangelized" once they have "heard." Success is defined, of course, in terms of the number of "decisions." Now that we have a measurable outcome, we are prepared to capitalize upon opportunity through use of secular strategic planning.

Without realizing what we have done, the gospel has too often been reduced to something analogous to a consumer product that can be mass marketed to demonstrate competitive superiority over alternative belief systems.[25] It is now feasible to utilize mass media such as television, literature and film consistent with secular advertising practices to build awareness and interest in product benefits.

Then individual Christians (the sales force) are motivated by various incentives to present (sell) the product and encourage its acceptance (sale).

Unfair? Of course, not everyone has bowed the knee to this pragmatic baal. Nevertheless, we contend that it is an appropriate description of evangelistic practice in many quarters around the globe. In our search for standardized *magic strategy keys*, we are all too willing to ignore that people come to faith in Christ through a uniquely personal decision process that takes place over time and is an outcome of multiple influences.[26] It is time to return to the example of Jesus who walked and lived among those whom he served—who took time to understand their spiritual awareness, fears and dreams through observation and listening. His strategy was unique to each situation and audience. We will have much more to say about this in the next chapter.

Tragically, this managerial reductionism short-circuits the theological cornerstone that the Holy Spirit alone is responsible for conviction, regeneration and sanctification (Jn 16:13-14; Rom 12:3; 1 Pet 1:2). By what authority can we establish measurable goals such as church growth or expected numbers of converts? Our quick tendency to cite statistical outcomes as indicators of *our "success"* only violates the fact that the most we can hope to accomplish through evangelistic strategy is to cooperate with the Spirit to help create an understanding of the gospel message sufficient to enable a person to grasp its implications for their life.

Having said all of this, however, we do believe that there are biblical principles that call for careful analysis, planning and evaluation. Consider John Stott's prophetic words:

> Some say rather piously that the Holy Spirit is himself the complete and satisfactory solution to the problem of communication, and indeed that when he is present and active, then communication ceases to be a problem. . . . Do we now have liberty to be as obscure, confused and irrelevant as we like, and the Holy Spirit will make all things plain? To use the Holy Spirit to rationalize our laziness is nearer blasphemy than piety.[27]

As we will contend in chapter four, Christians are participants in a dual process whereby we are expected to plan our course of action in full reliance on the Lord who determines our steps and outcomes (Prov 16:9). This is radically different from the secular world in which planners and strategists have full responsibility for goals, actions and outcomes. Christians, on the other hand, cannot assume sovereign control at any phase and still claim to be functioning within the providence of God. Therefore, we must exercise great caution in the use of secular planning models, a truth that seems to elude many architects of grand strategies for world evangelization.

A preoccupation with numerical success. It was not long after the Enlightenment before evangelicals were caught up in the common philosophy that *bigness is a sign of greatness.* In fact, quantifiable results became a virtual obsession, especially during this century in America. Donald A. McGavran, the founder of what is now known as church growth theory, contends that numerical church growth is the "chief and irreplaceable goal of world mission."[28] This premise was based on empirical observations in India that genuine conversion is expressed through church attendance. Therefore, following this line of reasoning, a growing church presumably is a successful church.

Many numerical growth advocates base their convictions on the fact that God is not willing for any to perish. Indeed we believe that all heaven rejoices when new believers are reached with the gospel. While it cannot be denied that love for all humankind is a basic attribute of God, we cannot discern any scriptural basis for the contention that "success" in Christian stewardship is reflected in numerical growth. In fact, we see just the opposite.

We must wrestle anew with the sober warning of Jesus that "small is the gate and narrow the road that leads to life, and only a few find it." (Mt 7:14). And we must consider the teaching of the parable of the soils that most who respond will fall away and not persevere. Indeed the early church, while vital in many ways, was small and often misdirected in both its life and outreach. Paul, in fact, seemed to feel at the end of his life that his labors in Asia had largely gone for naught (2 Tim 1:15). So numerical growth, in and of itself, ought not be the driving goal of our missions strategy.

The central goal of Jesus was to attract and empower a new generation of believers—admittedly only a receptive minority in a vast harvest field—who would spread his message as they follow a living Lord. His focus was on a style of life demonstrably different from the world at large, on quality rather than quantity. Numerical growth, if it occurs, is an *outcome of a church that is pure and blameless, not a goal in and of itself.*[29]

Matters are made even worse by our temptation to yield to syncretism in our desire to bring about positive responses. It is enticing, of course, to stress the worldly benefits offered from a relationship with Christ without stressing the costs. But in so doing we can easily compromise the integrity of the gospel. As Orlando Costas observed, "Instead of confronting people with the demands of Christ, the church has accommodated the gospel to their way of thinking and living."[30] There is no question that many will respond when this is done and even claim to be "Christian." But we build on a base of sand a house that is certain to collapse when challenged.

It is time to tone down the Christian public relations machinery that runs at fever pitch reporting the numbers allegedly reached through crusades, the electronic and print media, and intensified personal evangelism initiatives. Far too many claims of success are based on partial or misleading indicators, such as a focus on the number who come forward or who pray the sinner's prayer. All such actions can be motivated by many considerations apart from interest in the gospel.[31] In fact, one Japanese leader confided a number of years ago, "If we counted the number of reported conversions since the end of World War II, we would have more Christians than people." Need we say more?

An unhealthy relationship between numerical success and fundraising. Strategic planning designed to bring about numerical growth can be expensive, and it is rare to encounter a ministry plan that does not call for funds to be raised. As a result, churches and agencies in all parts of the world find themselves in competition for increasingly scarce financial resources. The Western model of capital-intensive, high-salaried ministry sustained by intensive fundraising has not been lost on our counterparts worldwide. Contrary to the model of Jesus and his disciples, the most frequently heard lament centers on the extent to which ministry is hampered by inadequate funds.

Not surprisingly, fundraising has assumed high priority in Christian ministry worldwide. In one sense, this is as it should be, because there is no denial of the Scriptural principle that financial generosity is an essential characteristic of authentic Christian life (see especially 2 Cor 8—9). Indeed a discerning disciple should wrestle more with the issue of the portion of earnings that should be spent in daily life as opposed to that returned through tithes and offerings.

Our concern is that today's preoccupation with fundraising has moved far from its biblical foundations. First of all, it is disturbing to observe the extent to which churches and agencies tend to lose sight of the basic principle that God expects his people to use the resources they have, no matter how meager, unless he directs differently (Phil 4:12-19). The tragic outcome all too often is a debilitating dependency on outside funding that virtually nullifies local initiative.[32]

Savvy marketers, furthermore, have become aware that contemporary donors, both individual and institutional, largely respond to what has become known as the "bang for the buck" appeal—the greater the numbers generated in a ministry that is of personal interest, the greater the motivation to give. Numerical outcomes thus become the primary way to assert competitive superiority over others, thereby increasing ministry revenues. Another cycle begins once these revenues are invested in ministry that is claimed to be successful. "Success" leads to more revenue, and on it goes.

Even worse, consider what happens when ministry needs do not match donor priorities. Legitimate causes, such as leadership development or social justice, may need to be downscaled or even abandoned because of low donor interest. Few ministries today, church or agency, are free from this dilemma. The temptation is to shift ministry gears in favor of other more "saleable" options because of the necessity to keep operating funds flowing through the door. Donors enamored with an erroneous "success mentality," especially large-scale institutional or major donors, need to be confronted with the very real likelihood that they could be guilty of "muzzling the ox" (Deut 25:4).

Recently Alex de Waal has described a phenomenon he calls "Humanitarian Gresham's Law."[33] According to this law, debased coinage without regulation will drive real coinage out of circulation. For example, a coin with only 50 percent silver will force all pure silver coins to be melted down into two coins. This law is applied in a very interesting way to humanitarian agencies seeking to raise funds from donors. Sooner or later, he argues, those who are willing to make compromises in truth and integrity to raise funds will drive all others out of business. It is quite possible that undue pandering to donor expectations, high numerical response being a case in point, will have exactly this outcome.

Reform is long overdue, and it must originate with those who ask for funds. As we make clear in chapter four, there must be willingness to take a decisive step away from donor-driven ministry and to place unquestioning faith in the Lord's commitment to provide all that we *legitimately* need. God has declared that the cattle on a thousand hills are his (Ps 50:10) and that he and he alone will provide for the needs of those who "seek first his kingdom and his righteousness" (Mt 6:33). It often is his plan to impress donors to respond with generosity, but *this decision must be motivated by the King, not by direct marketers.*

Displacement of the Local Church in World Outreach

A central theological reality is that the church is uniquely equipped to be the locus of missions because it is essentially missionary by its very nature.[34] This means that the church itself is the missionary reality that God's sends into the world—*it is far more than an institutional source from which funds and missionaries are sent or agency-developed programs carried out.* Indeed it is both the message and the medium expressing the fullness of the reign of Christ.

Paul argues that the church is "the aroma of Christ to God among those who are being saved and those who are perishing. To the one we are the smell of death; to the other, the fragrance of life. And who is equal to such a task? Unlike so many, we do not peddle the word of God for profit. On the contrary, in Christ we speak before God with sincerity, like men sent from God" (2 Cor 2:15-17). A better theological description of missions could not be imagined.

The missionary nature of the church both at home and on the field unfortunately has diminished in the last century because of the dramatic growth of missions agencies, often referred to today as being "parachurch." This has often been manifested in two particular ways: (1) missions efforts have been initiated by agencies who often have little accountability to the church and (2) missions agencies have fostered a superior-subordinate relationship with churches on the field.

An agency-initiated missions effort. Mission agencies historically have made it possible for otherwise isolated and ill-equipped local churches to participate in a dynamic presence on distant, inaccessible missions fields through providing wealth and missionary candidates. Indeed it was quite a challenge until recent times for a church to fulfill its missionary vision and responsibility beyond its own Jerusalem. Missionary agencies, as they were developed in the nineteenth century, thus played an important role. But conditions soon changed dramatically. Independent missions agencies were often formed in the twentieth century because the mainline denominations had given up on missions. While they were clearly called by God to fill a growing vacuum, they risked marginalizing the local church.

The movement of forming missions agencies outside of church structures accelerated between World War I and World War II and has increased exponentially since 1945. In 1990 it was estimated that older denominations were providing only 5 percent of all missionaries. Today the vast majority of missionaries being sent out are being sent by interdenominational missions.[35] Therefore a large and diverse North American institutional missions presence (Mission, Inc.) emerged which is dominant in nearly all parts of the world. In this structure, local churches have been expected to play only the passive role of support providers.

The technological revolution following World War II, however, opened the worldwide door for the local church as never before. A whole generation emerged that was freed from the isolation of its parents, thus planting the seeds for what now has become a resurgence of local church interest in crossing cultural boundaries in initiatives that often have little or no relationship with Mission, Inc.[36]

What this means, in short, is that parachurch agencies now are joined by local church initiatives ranging from partnerships between churches and agencies to the formation of church-based programs that in effect become agencies in their own right. Not surprisingly, tension and misunderstanding often can arise. But these realities, if anything, will intensify. Our next two chapters are a serious attempt to address the issues that must be faced if both mission agencies and local churches are to share a vital ministry.

A superior-subordinate relationship with churches on the field. Most missions initiatives in modern times have been dedicated to church planting, accompanied by a genuine desire to see these new entities grow and thrive. As we stress in every chapter, we acknowledge and affirm a remarkable worldwide Christian presence that otherwise would have been impossible. Unfortunately, there also has been a widespread tendency within evangelicalism to conceptualize the local church primarily as a *medium* for evangelism to reach a lost world—a means by which the bare "message" of the gospel is to be transmitted.

The problem intensifies when agencies are tempted to view the local church on the field as simply a convenient vehicle through which their own evangelistic aspirations are to be fulfilled. Barrett and Reapsome identified 788 global plans for world evangelization with 250 active as of 1988, and that number no doubt burgeoned in the following decade.[37] A large proportion of these are designed with the goal of enlisting local church participation through such incentives as training, finances and pastoral recognition.

Those who utilize the local church in this way often are well meaning, and it cannot be denied that fresh spiritual vitality and power sometimes comes from outside. But we must respectfully point out, as we emphasized in the last chapter, that the source of power and momentum has shifted away from the West. In other words, churches that were infants in earlier generations now have grown to adulthood and are demanding recognition that they alone have primary authority and responsibility to extend God's kingdom where they are. Anything that creates or encourages dependence on outside initiatives abrogates this divine obligation. There is no question that the local church is central to God's program. God intended the church to *be* his message and not simply carry it.

Fortunately, we are hearing from the grassroots in the Two-Thirds World a groundswell of protest that such practices represent little more than disguised imperialism undercutting and even demeaning local initiative. Like a mustard seed, the kingdom is locally rooted and is extended as these particular cells of the worldwide body grow and multiply through their own initiative. Over time there will be a powerful presence, a quiet reality devoid of human power and grandeur, bearing the fruit of salvation and accompanied by miracles, healing, justice and relief from oppression. We are reminded of the tree of life envisioned initially in the Garden of Eden and painted even more boldly in the second chapter of Daniel.

This is not to say that missions agencies have no valid role. Indeed God can and does raise up such entities, first of all, when the church draws into itself and abrogates its responsibility. Furthermore, specialized services and ministries can augment and expand churches with what they cannot do by themselves. Our objection enters when agencies, especially those from the West, exercise such power through their funds and expertise that they assume dominance in world missions. When this happens, the arm controls the body in a unwarranted manner. The need is for responsible partnership whereby agencies (the arms) serve the body in constructive ways. Note that we are not calling for independence but for mutual service.

To underline the diversity of missions opportunities that coexist in a local church, consider this. The scruffy musician who has recently started attending your church may well have a tattooed girlfriend who is running one of the one-hundred-plus Christian tattoo parlors that have sprung up across America. These parlors have formed their own association that exists to encourage the development of these parlors as missions outposts—perhaps today's equivalent of missions preaching points!

At the same time, sitting a few rows in front of these young people may be some young professionals who have made a great deal of money as venture capitalists or through corporate stock options. Groups of these professionals are currently banding together in various places around the world to combine their assets in support of Christian missions opportunities. These seem certain to put our faith promise strategies in the shade. Such is the character of our postmodern world, and *these changed circumstances demand a change in structure.*

Breaking Free from the Shackles of Modernity

Now we are back to James Morey's question as he met with the missions board of First Church of Rollingwood: *What's gone wrong with the harvest?* We hope that the answer is now clear. The root cause of a growing world church that seems to be listing in the spiritual waters is simply this: *Our Western churches and agencies are still functioning in a world missions mindset established well over one hundred years ago. Furthermore, we have infected a world church with the disease of modernity through our failure to discern the signs of the times decades ago. As a result, we are bordering on the very edge of being judged as unworthy to carry the mantle God once placed on North American missions.*

Mark Noll has well identified this problem as "the scandal of the evangelical mind." As he put it, we evangelicals held on to the basic Christian truths by fleeing from the problems of a world immersed in modernity, into a fascination with inner spirituality and the details of end times prophecy.[38] We all but abdicated the public sector of society in our single-minded focus on the spiritual lifeboat provided by evangelism and powered by strategic thinking and technology. To make matters worse, the potent model of Jesus as a patient discipler and mentor has largely been overlooked—it seems that holy living and the other fruits of the Spirit are assumed to follow once conversion takes place.

Furthermore, we have confidently carried out our donor-driven strategic plans for world evangelization. We have attracted much attention in the process, but where is the harvest? Large numbers have claimed to become Christian, but where is the evidence of the reign of Christ that always accompanies genuine Spirit-led outreach?

Continuation with business as usual is not an option for those who claim to be following the Lord of the Harvest who desires us to live with biblical fidelity and wisdom. Churches and agencies alike must start by putting everything under scrutiny in a spirit of joining with Jesus where he always has been—at the very forefront and cutting edge of the kingdom's advance.

So what is the solution? It is both simple and terrifying—*it's time to admit our captivity to outmoded paradigms*. We have steered through decades of modernity with scarce recognition of its contaminating effects. And now our dilemma is greatly intensified as we begin to come to grips with the worldview known as *postmodernism*.

We have been arguing that we are now in a wholly different situation from that in which modern missions began and developed. The center of Christianity is no longer to be found in the West; indeed, Christianity has become widely dispersed throughout the world. Signs of life and vitality have sprung up on every continent, and many centers of missions are now operative.

This new situation calls for a new kind of missions structure, which we have characterized as mutual exchange between multiple centers of influence and varieties of gifts, and it demands a new holism that returns to the biblical call to bring the whole of life under the authority of Christ.

In the remaining chapters we will develop this into a new paradigm of world missions. This paradigm is generated by Jesus' own mission statement—*it is the establishment and extension of God's kingdom and reign on this earth*. In most respects, it is not new at all. In fact, it can be argued that God's eternal plan called for establishing his kingdom and reign through his son, Jesus Christ, who came to earth as Lord over all of creation, reconciling all things to himself (Col 1:15-20). His goal was to establish a "radiant church, without stain or wrinkle or any other blemish, but holy and blameless" (Eph 5:27).

As we see it, this *kingdom paradigm* should have these characteristics:

☐ *Obedience to the entirety of Christ's Great Commission.* Evangelism will once again be viewed as only the first step in an ongoing process of reaching the lost and making disciples through baptizing all who respond (Mt 28:18-20) and teaching them to "produce fruit in keeping with repentance" (Mt 3:8).

☐ *Dedication to ongoing initiatives to plant and build churches that model and proclaim the good news through their words (1 Pet 3:15) and their lifestyle of personal holiness exemplified by Jesus Christ.* The local church is God's chosen means for spreading the gospel through a ministry that radiates outward and multiplies from cells of the kingdom. This will take place only when churches are conceived as an organism built around community, which provides a genuine witness to a living Christ and presents an authentic and appealing option to those living by the standards of the world (Eph 5:1-21).

☐ *Establishment of alliances that cross international borders so that kingdom resources may be combined and mobilized in mutual centers of influence to spread the kingdom to the whole world.* Agencies such as missions boards will be welcomed to the extent that they provide resources and specialized skills as equal partners with no intent to control outcomes.

☐ *Strategies to extend the kingdom by infiltrating all segments of society, with preference given to the poor, and allowing no dichotomy between evangelism and social transformation (Lk 4:18-19).*

☐ *Evangelism understood and embraced as the outcome of a lifestyle centered in true empathy based on love, genuine respect and willingness to address the deepest longings of others with the good news of Jesus (1 Pet 3:15).*

☐ *Restored understanding of God's people as co-laborers created by him to carry out his works (1 Cor 3:9; Eph 2:10).* Revitalized prayer will seek specific guidance and direction that can come through the Holy Spirit, who illuminates all truth and reveals what is yet to come (Jn 16:13-14). The people of God, in turn, will assume enlightened responsibility for stewardship that is ensured by strategic thinking, proper management of resources and ongoing evaluation.

In short, missions in a postmodern world will, in our opinion, be church-centered, focusing on strengthening and empowering God's people. The message of the gospel will once again be envisioned as a holistic one expressed through words and authenticated by the salt and light coming from genuine community (Mt 5:13-16). Individual initiatives will give way to networking, whereby strengths are complemented as Christians think, work and pray together to extend the reign of Christ.

We are encouraged by the newly emerging worldview represented by the bearded, scruffy-looking rock musician of Bob Fryling's story. This new paradigm has come to be termed postmodern, since in many respects it has developed in reaction to the pretentious claims of modernity.

As often captured in the lyrics of popular music, this generation has grown disillusioned with the universalistic claims of reason and with the large impersonal institutions that have grown up in the service of the claims of reason and rational methods. Moreover they have recovered a deep longing for the sacred in their lives and a desire to integrate religion (or at least spirituality) into the whole of their lives. As a result there is a new openness to religious claims and a deep desire to be involved in changing the world. We maintain that these sensitivities, though they are not without their own dangers, provide a unique opportunity for missions that we must not miss.

In the pages that follow, we will attempt within our own limitations to help you sharpen your ability to diagnose the signs of the times and to respond in a creative way as you discern what the Spirit is saying and sense where the Spirit is guiding. So stay with us, because once we break loose from the shackles of the past, we are free once again to do all things through Christ who strengthens us. But be prepared: that scruffy, bearded young man and his tattooed girlfriend in the back row may be among your most valuable assets for missions!

4

....

Missions in a Postmodern World
A Gracious Revolution

*The senior staff at Global Harvest Mission (GHM) soon found them-*selves part of this exciting discovery process through the infectious influence of James Morey. It came together in a very exciting way for Bud Anderson, general director, one night when he was returning from the West Coast on a long plane flight. Here are his words to the staff at their next weekly chapel.

"I was sitting by the window at the very front of the coach cabin on one of the clearest nights I have ever seen. There was some moonlight, but there were no clouds at all. As I looked down over the plains states, I was impressed at how clearly I saw dots of light scattered everywhere. And I thought back on my childhood on the farm and realized that these must have been yard lights. I remember how warm and friendly a yard light was. It gave me a sense of safety and belonging in what otherwise was a pretty scary world.

"As I watched this panorama, I saw other places where there were clusters of light. These were small towns and settlements where there were many lights. And I saw how much more the light pushed back the darkness, even to the point that I almost could make out details on the ground. As I pondered this wonderful sight, I suddenly had the strong impression that I was receiving a vivid picture of what the reign of Christ really is. I saw the individual lights as small pockets of believers, maybe even one person, spreading light where they were. And the settlements were ever so much brighter because of many lights.

"Then, with clear insight, I saw how the reign of Christ and his kingdom is extended. It happens one light at a time. And I saw that the light had to be the very light of Jesus himself in the lives of his people. One light at a time. Then my eyes dropped to the latest field reports on my lap. Hundreds of converts here, thousands there through our mass evangelism. But I was reminded how many times I have gone into these 'reached' areas only to see very little light in spite of our numbers.

"Do we need a fresh vision of why we exist? We are called to multiply these lights—mature believers—worldwide, to show the way to a world consumed with personal gain. We have made many converts but few disciples. And we have confidently reported our numbers and have forgotten that the only real evidence that disciples have been made is through clear signs that the very life of Jesus is being seen through his people in our churches."

Yes, points of light, or "patches of green in the desert," as Philip Yancey puts it.[1] The kingdom and reign of Christ expands within society through salt and through light, changing it from the inside out as Christians bring the grace of God to the world where they live. It takes place almost imperceptibly through ordinary people, transformed by their Lord, on a journey or pilgrimage with him. This constitutes the meaning of the reign of Christ—*common people transformed by their Lord doing uncommon deeds.* These points of light all illuminate the grace of Jesus Christ, the unbounded love of God for all of creation.

Fortunately the light of the reign of Christ is far from extinguished. Its impact is seldom glamorous and worthy of headlines, although there are great and noteworthy revivals at times. Furthermore, it rarely happens through large, heavily funded strategic initiatives, although these too have their role when undertaken by those who have broken free from the inroads of modernity. It takes place when we honor Christ's goal to establish a "radiant church, without stain or wrinkle or any other blemish, but holy and blameless" (Eph 5:27)—a church characterized by the deep moral and social changes that occur when believers truly follow the King.

*   *   *

IT IS OUR INTENT IN THIS CHAPTER TO HELP LAUNCH WHAT OUR friend and colleague Jim Plueddemann, general director of SIM, has referred to as "a gracious revolution in our thinking about world missions—not an angry, destructive revolution, but a loving revolution."[2] A new paradigm is needed that restores our Lord's mandate to make disciples among all peoples, disciples who manifest the full reality of the reign of Christ.

In the following pages, as well as the remaining chapters, we will advocate the *kingdom paradigm of world missions* described in chapter three.[3] It will differ sharply from the prevailing managerial paradigm, an outgrowth of modernity, in both its underlying theological premises and its methodology.

Actually the kingdom paradigm is not a newcomer on the scene. Rather, it is an embodiment of scriptural truths as reflected in ancient creeds of the church. What makes it radical is that it represents a direct challenge to modernity, which has so deeply invaded much of our missions enterprise today.

In this type of discussion it always is easy to attack the status quo, but it is something else again to propose an alternative that moves beyond pious platitudes and comes to grips with world realities. But amidst the uncertainty we have a strong sense of direction and many wonderful teachers. We invite you to come along as pilgrims, if you will, who are seeking to understand how together we can endeavor to follow Jesus and make his reign in his kingdom a more visible and potent reality.

Paradigms in Conflict

Once he finished his chapel message, Bud Anderson hurried to the GHM conference room for the beginning of what was to be many long hours of meetings with his six regional directors from around the world. His prepared agenda was to undergo radical alteration in the days that followed, because his words in chapel struck an unexpectedly powerful chord in the lives of all who were in attendance.

Clark Miller, Africa regional director, was the first to speak. "Bud," he said, "you have really helped me understand the uneasiness I have felt over our 'adopt a people group program.'" In the course of fifteen minutes, Clark reflected on the excitement this team had felt nearly four years ago when they, along with other missions and agencies around the world, were challenged to focus on people groups around the world where the gospel has not been preached. After prayer and discussion, six different groups were adopted on two continents. Clark recalled the exact words Bud expressed at that time: "At long last we are on the verge of fulfilling the Great Commission. The way is cleared for the coming of the Lord in the new millennium."

Bud winced as he heard these words. He was aware that a few churches had been planted among three of the groups, whereas a whole series of obstacles prevented further progress. First, there was resistance from missionaries in established fields who had been encouraged to leave their life's labor and become part of this pioneering effort. Furthermore, donors simply had not responded to a series of appeals to make this step a financial reality. He had to admit to his team that each of these initiatives had fallen short of the optimistic goals that were set and that the months of strategic planning had born little fruit.

*   *   *

The dilemma that Bud and his international leadership team faced can be traumatic indeed. Each person around that table was forced to ask, "Where did we go wrong?" All the members of this team have a rich educational background plus years of experience.

Certainly they do not lack the missiological understanding and skills that are felt to be essential in tackling today's challenges. What's more, they have worked together productively over a period of many years without similar setbacks. So what has gone wrong?

The Outcomes of Managerial Missiology

We see in this situation a legitimate attempt by a group of well-meaning leaders in GHM to respond to contemporary missiological thinking, which embodies measurable goals, precision, predictability and control. Their heart motivation unquestionably is to be effective stewards in God's vineyard. As they wrestle with the issue that Clark raised, they will realize they have adopted a strategic planning outlook that, when taken to its logical conclusion, is far removed from the model of Jesus.

Let us make perfectly clear that rationality and problem solving are consistent with the will of a creator God who said, "Let us make man in our image and in our likeness" (Gen 1:26). How else could we be stewards over all of God's creation unless we too were given the ability, although limited, to be creative and productive? Good stewards will logically turn to the world of business, politics and public administration to glean insights that might help them be more effective.

The dilemma begins, however, when we yield to the implications of the basic underlying premise of secular strategic planning: *rational thinking, informed by the rigor and logic of the scientific method, will inevitably lead to solutions to the problems that have always beset humankind.* This model, after all, has given rise to the technological age, even to the point that we have explored outer space and brought about unprecedented growth in standards of living. *Why not harness this power for God through entrepreneurial initiative?*

Indeed it *is* legitimate to harness this power for missions as long as we hold firmly to God's mandate that everything be done in accord with his word and motivated and empowered by the Holy Spirit. In short, *we are not expected to be autonomous problem solvers;* human reasoning in and of itself will not reveal God's perspective. And, in sharp contrast to business entrepreneurs who assume total responsibility for long-term, sustained profitability, God and God alone is responsible for the outcome of those who labor in his vineyard, not the leaders and workers themselves.

Losing sight of these foundational spiritual truths, our strategic planning becomes *managerial missiology.*[4] One day we awake to find that we have strayed far from all that God intends. We have found ourselves in precisely the dilemma the GHM team is facing for largely the same reasons. Well-meaning Christians burdened by a heart desire to reach the lost turn their missions pilgrimage in a direction that can have devastating consequences.

The starting point in this direction lies in a struggle to redefine our ministry challenge in such a way that specific outcomes can be discerned and assessed. This is quite a challenge in the context of the Great Commission. How can we ever know when all people groups have been discipled? If we cannot measure this outcome, how can we be more effective in fulfilling all that Jesus has asked us to do?

Now the entrepreneurial engines start turning and find traction on the ground prepared by modernity over the last one hundred years. During this time the Great Commission began to be conceived as a call to convert the maximum number of people in the shortest period of time. Evangelistic effectiveness began to be assessed in terms of the numbers who have been "reached" and have overtly responded.

The entrepreneurial project of missions retooled at the middle of the twentieth century when church growth theory made its entrance. This theory contends that numerical church growth is both a legitimate goal and an expected outcome. Missions strategy took a quantum leap forward with the computer technology of the information age, which made it possible to rapidly assess and disseminate vast quantities of information on unreached peoples worldwide. This launched a great "countdown," assessing numerical progress in reaching the unreached, which presumably reveals that most of the world will have been evangelized by the dawn of the new millennium.[5]

Churches and agencies worldwide were being mobilized to

achieve this goal in the shortest possible period of time. And ambitious strategic plans were launched and funded by missions-
minded Christians. We cannot deny that world missions has been
intensified and focused by today's strategic initiatives, and we
applaud the growth of a Christian presence worldwide. Yet we
respectfully submit that something indeed has gone wrong.

To sum up our discussion in earlier chapters, the redefinition of
the Great Commission to a measurable objective of maximizing
numbers of converts and church members has emasculated Christ's
imperative to make disciples in all nations. Jim Plueddemann puts it
well: "When we aim only at what we can measure, we ignore the
most important goals of character, discipleship and holiness, which
we cannot predict or quantify without falling into legalism . . . luke-
warm churches are the result of this assembly line mindset."[6]

Furthermore, today's prevailing focus on "completion of the
Great Commission" is a misleading call for humans to activate an
outcome that can only occur when Christ returns and gathers all
believers unto himself (Mt 24:30-31). The initiative in Christian outreach comes from God and God alone, not from fertile strategic
minds (Jn 5:17, 19-20); "For it is God who works in you to will and
to act according to his good purpose" (Phil 2:13). We cannot initiate
strategic outcomes and celebrate apparent success for which God
and God alone has responsibility.

Numerical growth, if it occurs at all, is an outcome brought by a
sovereign God who activates conviction, regeneration and sanctification (Jn 3:6-8; 16:8-11; Acts 1:8). God often calls the best people to
work in places where results, humanly speaking, are meager.

Now let's return to Bud Anderson, Clark Rogers and the rest of
the leadership team at GHM. It is easy to lose sight of the fact that
God will always honor the humble attitude of his servants. It was
not their motive, after all, to stray from the teachings of Jesus. Nonetheless they, along with many others, had fallen under the spell of
the spirit of modernity. Now a loving and patient God was speaking
to his servants and was about to lead them to a radically new and
fruitful paradigm of missions. Their listening and open hearts were
a gateway to a new beginning.

World Missions from a Kingdom Perspective
The goal of Christ's Great Commission is not simply to provide a lifeboat for lost souls. It is nothing less than creation of *communities of common people doing uncommon deeds*. Does this sound unrealistic? Of course. But perhaps this is because our thinking has been infected by nonscriptural patterns? We mobilize to "finish the task" (a concept alien to the teachings of Jesus), in a specific time period to hasten Christ's return (even Jesus did not know this timetable), with massive donor-driven evangelism (something foreign and actually opposed in the New Testament).

Let us remind ourselves, as we noted in the last chapter, how much this is like the secular institutions that modernity spawned. In those contexts, eschatology became a secular process that moved toward broad goals and dreams inspired by Western civilization itself—a *humanity come of age*. Soon we were to see vast organizations based on visions of world progress—the League of Nations, which later become the United Nations, the World Bank and the International Monetary Fund. These were structurally unified with strong, centralized control and driven by rational methodologies. Notice how Christians have done much the same thing in our determination to win the world in this generation.

What strategies will better reflect our contemporary postmodern situation? It is our contention that the time has come to return to the strategy of Jesus, who said he would build his church—dynamic communities that are (1) sensitive to the initiative of God, (2) motivated by a vision of the reign of Christ refracted through the multiple cultures of the world, (3) characterized by mutual sharing from multiple centers of influence, and (4) committed to partnership and collaboration.

Communities sensitive to the initiative of God. Jesus provided a clear model for missions by his actions and words. This model sharply contradicts the rationalistic assumption of secular strategic planning models. Carefully consider his words:

> "My Father is always at his work to this very day, and I, too, am working. . . . I tell you the truth, the Son can do nothing by himself. He can do only what he sees his Father doing, because whatever the

Father does the Son also does. For the Father loves the Son and shows him all he does." (Jn 5:17, 19-20)

Later, Jesus added this astonishing encouragement, "I tell you the truth, anyone who has faith in me will do what I have been doing. He will do even greater things than these, because I am going to the Father" (Jn 14:12).

The strategic implications? Henry Blackaby and Claude King capture their essence with clarity and power:

> God takes the initiative to involve His people with Him in His work. He does this on His timetable, not on ours. He is the One who is already at work in our world. When He opens your spiritual eyes to see where He is at work, that revelation is your invitation to join Him. You will know where He is working when you see Him doing things that only God can do. When God reveals His work to you, that is the time He wants you to begin adjusting to Him and His activity. What God purposes, He Himself guarantees its completion.[7]

All our planning and practice then must be responsive to what God has already begun. Suffused with patient discernment and prayer, it reflects an attitude of listening to God and his people. All of our efforts must be undertaken in humility. We are to be faithful and careful listeners to what God and others are saying. To paraphrase Karl Barth, *missions, like theology, is primarily a matter of prayer and answer to prayer.*

The most difficult challenge in the kingdom paradigm of world missions is to discern God's voice in directing and guiding our actions. Secular strategic planning always begins with focused research to reveal opportunities and challenges. This then is interpreted by skilled planners, drawing upon past experience and intuition to glean creative insights.

We don't want to say that research is unnecessary for Christian strategists. Jesus himself was a careful listener and observer who took into account the backgrounds and needs of those whom he encountered. He met people on the hillsides, in the streets, in the fields, at work, at prayer, at weddings, on the road. He lived, walked and talked with them. The apostle Paul followed in his footsteps as he discerned patterns of communication and influence in the Roman Empire.

The difficulty enters, however, in interpreting observational and survey research in such a way as to discern where God is at work. The massive database on unreached people provides a relevant example. Clearly there is a compelling, biblical mandate to bring Christian presence into the lives of those who have had no opportunity to hear the good news. But *the existence of need in and of itself does not signify a call to ministry!* Jesus himself healed and responded to only a *minority* of those he encountered, the woman at the well and the blind beggar being pertinent examples. He responded, in turn, only when the Father revealed through prayer that he was already at work in their lives. The call of Jesus, then, was to join the Father where he was already at work.

Was God calling the GHM community of missionaries to adopt the six unreached people groups they chose? Who knows? Often the urgency of the situation overwhelms the voice of God. Furthermore, what would you say if you discovered that these decisions were made after a veteran senior leader proclaimed with passion and conviction that "God has shown me that these six are his target for us"? While God can speak in this way, and this is one way to discern where God is leading, leaders are, after all, fallible human beings. History is full of Christian initiatives undertaken in full conviction but that later proved to be unwise.

Every claim to have heard God's voice must be carefully examined. The first step is to ascertain that the so-called "leading" is consistent with Scripture. If not, it should be questioned. Then it always is wise to consult others facing similar challenges. Scripture makes clear that "plans fail for lack of counsel, but with many advisors they succeed" (Prov 15:22). The second step is to establish what resources are available to take the action that is contemplated. When a mission agency discovers, after careful planning and prayer, for example, that a national church has also targeted the same group, we can have greater confidence that God is putting the pieces together.

Communities motivated by a vision of the reign of Christ. Christ's followers are empowered and unleashed to follow in his steps to make demonstrable differences in the lives of others both within the church and in the world at large. In our zeal for making the maximum number of converts, we have all but lost sight of this foundational principle.

It is helpful once again to view the reign of Christ as manifesting itself in ever-growing points of light in a dark world. While an individual believer can indeed be a point of light, God created his church as the means to focus and extend this light. A healthy church, after all, is a community of those whose allegiance lies with Jesus Christ. The body, as a whole, is a supernaturally empowered and motivated entity, which by its corporate behavior gives a very clear message to the world. Gradually, this light spreads and illumines a whole community. In so doing, the message of the reign of Jesus becomes compellingly evident, even without an overt strategy of persuasion.

One point of light with a small beginning in Victorian England was the Clapham Sect, a tiny group of believers, including Charles Simeon and William Wilberforce, who succeeded in electing five of its members to Parliament.[8] Through their determined efforts over time, slavery was abolished, prison reforms were introduced, housing was provided for the poor, child labor was opposed, and there were movements against public immorality and drunkenness. Opponents mocked them with the label "saints," which they proudly wore. Because of the light of Christ, they helped change the way of life for an entire nation.

Contemplate the scenario, however, of an institutionalized church such as First Church of Rollingwood, drawn in on itself, largely failing to do the *uncommon deed* throughout its community. Even if it should undertake door-to-door evangelism or launch crusades, it would have little effect other than indifference. It is not a radiant church, with the result that it essentially has little impact on the community.

Here we see the utter barrenness of yielding to the worldview of modernity, which separates our personal and private concerns from the public "real world." Ron Sider hits this issue squarely when he observes, "It is surely astonishing that precisely those Christians who speak most often about their desire to be biblical and their passion for evangelism do not define the gospel the way Jesus did."[9] Evangelism may build a lifeboat—even a very large lifeboat—but this may ignore the example of Jesus and have little or no impact on institutional sin and injustice. Remember the prophetic observation of Os Guinness that the church has lost its message by "becoming privately engaging, socially irrelevant."[10]

The reign of Christ demands biblical holism, which restores the indivisible unity between the personal and the public, between evangelism and social transformation. As Peter Kuzmič puts it, it is time for "servants of the King to excel in righteousness and practice a prophetic spirituality."[11] Christians over the last three decades have responded to this challenge by developing three perspectives on how social transformation can be integrated with evangelism: (1) it is a *consequence* of evangelism; (2) it is a *bridge* to evangelism, or (3) it is a *full partner* with evangelism.

The first of these, a *consequence* of evangelism, is largely based on the social impact of widespread conversion and revival prior to the entry of modernity into the church around 1850. The evidence is clear, however, that since then social transformation has *not* followed evangelism except in isolated instances.[12]

Social transformation as a *bridge to evangelism* is unquestionably a step in the right direction. It nonetheless represents a reductionist approach that grossly violates the example of Jesus by relegating ministries of compassion and justice to little more than a component of evangelistic strategy, or to pre-evangelism.

Version three, *partnership*, affirms that evangelism and social transformation are inseparable elements in Christ's kingdom that embraces all of creation (Lk 4:18-20). The goal is *shalom*—a sense of human welfare and well-being that transcends an artificial distinction between the private and public worlds.[13] Shalom, by its very nature, is rooted in justice and compassion.[14]

In our opinion, partnership is the only option if we take the reign of Christ and the lessons of church history seriously. We agree with John Stott's contention that "what is needed now is the development of more innovative models of integrated mission, in which the Gospel, far from being silenced or marginalized by social involvement, is illuminated and enforced by it."[15] Unless this step is taken, Christianity is all but stripped of anything other than privatistic relevance.

Communities characterized by mutual sharing from multiple centers of influence. The reign of Christ will assume wonderfully varied shapes wherever it is expressed and empowered by the Spirit. The Clapham Sect responded to the needs of its time and place; Christians today in, say South Africa, face vastly different challenges since the fall of apartheid. As a result, theology and missiology can no longer be understood as a single product, developed in the centers of missiological power in the West and duly exported elsewhere.

There is no question in today's postmodern world that the concept of a *center* (the haves) and *periphery* (the have-nots) is barren and outmoded. Wealth, technology and power are *not* determining missiological considerations. Missions thrives when it overflows from true Christian community. Only then is there a message with authentic credibility.

It is not surprising in this context that the momentum in world missions has definitively shifted to the Two-Thirds World, where many in our former missions fields at the "periphery" have taken up the mantle of Jesus Christ in a demonstrable and powerful way. There is a clear identification with Jesus, who never deviated from his life mission statement in Luke 4 to announce the good news and minister to the poor and the oppressed.

☐ Christian witness emanates, as it should, from the grassroots outward through a community of believers whose corporate life consistently bears the fruit of the Spirit, thereby providing an authentic and winsome embodiment of the gospel. Here is the basis for a credible prophetic message.

☐ Seeds are planted and brought into life as ordinary people follow the model of their Lord in daily life, always seeking to provide a reason for the hope that is within them.

☐ Believers function as true pilgrims, inviting the lost to join them on a journey as part of a community of pilgrims who have found a hope and a source of power that transcends the secular and material.

☐ This witness, while small and almost indiscernible, grows in power and impact as a single point of light expands into multiple points of light. Incarnate witness in the form of new communities of Christians will embody the reign of Christ and its justice.

☐ Outcomes are assessed by discernible changes in individual lives, in society and in the church. Numbers are not a motivating consideration.

There is much to be learned from the model given by Jesus, where his mission was carried out from Galilee to Jerusalem.[16] As you will recall from earlier chapters, Galilee at the time of Jesus was largely the home of the despised and the rejected. Jesus made his base among the poor and oppressed by establishing a messianic community with a radical ministry that challenged the very roots of the corrupt power structure in Jerusalem. In so doing, he established his credentials by a disavowal of wealth, social status and power. It is small wonder that he was welcomed by the masses and scorned by the elite as he unmasked their corruption and hypocrisy.

Jesus further clarifies what he meant by this strategy when he prays, "I praise you, Father, Lord of heaven and earth, because you have hidden these things from the wise and learned, and revealed them to little children" (Mt 11:25). His message is clear—those who are captivated with all the world can offer also become imprisoned to its value system. The message of Jesus only makes sense to those who have come to see the comparative worthlessness of all that they have held dear.

Missions, therefore, requires a fundamental association and identification with the most marginalized, because the essence of the good news is liberation, justice and shalom. One of the most exciting examples of this comes from Spain, a country where true believers are considered to be an irrelevant Christian remnant.[17] There among the gypsies we have an ideal example of contemporary disciples who are a disenfranchised and reviled minority, serving as the catalyst for a surprising movement of God. Without fanfare and publicity, the kingdom grows from the mustard seeds they represent.

Communities committed to partnership and collaboration. Chapter two highlighted a unique aspect of Paul's ministry, when he called for a wide scale Christian collaboration to meet the basic survival needs of the church in Jerusalem. The Christian communities that he established, in other words, were not conceived as isolated and autonomous points of light. Rather they were expected to combine their resources in service to the Lord.

Unfortunately the Protestant church and its agencies since the days of the Reformation have been characterized by division, lack of unity and even internal hostility. The message of Jesus has been corrupted by competitiveness, evident today as agencies clamor for the donor dollar on the basis of their individual successes. While there are notable exceptions, which we thankfully acknowledge, the principle of interdependence discussed in chapter two is scarcely evident in many quarters.

Today we need a truly global conversation and collaboration, where everyone will be heard, and all will learn together.[18] Fortunately there is a healthy move toward mission alliances made up of agencies and churches, both indigenous and expatriate, which have recognized the synergistic impact when the body joins hands. We especially applaud the healthy initiatives of Phill Butler and his colleagues at Interdev.[19]

We must point out, however, that an unfortunate spirit of expatriate missionary imperialism often infuses alliances and partnerships between Western entities and their Two-Thirds World counterparts. When the outsider brings finances and other resources to the table, it is too easy for the one who pays the piper to call the tune. In other words, the outsider drives the program.

A spirit of partnership and collaboration is further eroded when any participant assumes a dominant role and is unwilling to function in submission to others. Once again, missions representatives often are the offenders because, whether intentionally or not, they take the posture of those who "have" coming to those who "have not." Without a spirit of mutual submission and interdependency, collaboration will die.

At this exciting stage of history, Western mission agencies no longer can consider themselves to be in the "driver's seat." In fact, quite the opposite is true in such countries as Ghana, India and Brazil, to mention just three of many. In short, the infant has become an adult and is demanding a "Paul-Barnabas" relationship rather than a "Paul-Timothy" relationship based on one being subordinate to the other.

Today those who come from the outside must come alongside their counterparts with a desire to facilitate and enable all that those onsite are trying to accomplish, to see what "value" can be added from their presence. They must be sensitive, in other words, both to what God is already doing there and to the capabilities God has raised up in that place. The West is in a wonderful position to provide leadership development and specialized skills. But these must be offered with no strings attached and an authentic affirmation that we are equal partners with no desire to control or influence. We will address this important issue in more detail in chapter six.

Discerning and responding strategically to the voice of the Holy Spirit. It is time to flesh out what world missions might look like if it is (1) initiated and empowered by God, (2) motivated by a vision of the reign of Christ, (3) characterized by mutual sharing from multiple centers of influence, and (4) committed to partnership and collaboration. The guiding vision is to establish and extend points of light, communities of Christian believers, who are following their Lord as he establishes and extends his spiritual kingdom.

Rather than following a managerial paradigm of ministry, followers of Jesus should be motivated in their service by a vision of the reign of Christ. They should have a sharp sense of purpose and direction based on a keen understanding of their world as seen through the eyes of Jesus. They should dream dreams and think strategically, intending to discern where the Lord is working and then join him. The model of Jesus as disclosed by his life and words is their guide.

In this kingdom paradigm of world missions, those we consider to be unreached are not viewed as candidates or customers for the gospel. Rather, our objective is to invite others, believers and nonbelievers, to join us in a pilgrimage to discover the reality of a risen

Lord. As Jim Plueddemann puts it, ministry is driven by

> a vision of what it could do for the people, for the church, and for
> society. . . . Lost people are invited to join them on the road to Christ,
> to involve them in a community of believers, and help them to
> become all God intends them to be. They challenge them to follow the
> map of the Word and to become life-long obedient students of Jesus.[20]

The Spiritual Pilgrimage Model

The kingdom paradigm embraces the basic premise that everyone,
believer or nonbeliever, is on a spiritual pilgrimage that does not
end in this lifetime but consummates only upon the return of Christ.
To use the wonderful analogy of John Bunyan's classic *Pilgrim's
Progress*, all are seekers with a deep hunger, a prevailing restless-
ness, to find meaning and authenticity. Our call is to join them on
this road right where they are and point them to Jesus. As Blackaby
and King put it, "The only way people will know what God is like is
when they see Him at work. They know His nature when they see
His nature expressed in His activity. . . . Let the world see God at
work and He will attract people to Himself."[21]

The journey. God's message is one of hope and of love. He created
the universe and populated it with humans for just one reason—he
desired an intimate, loving relation with all whom he created. This
great vision, of course, has been opposed by human disobedience
and by spiritual forces opposed to God.

The entire course of biblical history is the story of a grieving God,
longing for the return of his beloved people, even to the point that
he sends his Son to establish his spiritual kingdom, his divine lordship, through those who follow Christ and become his body the
church. And by Christ's death, God paves the way for a return to an
intimate and loving relationship for all who choose to follow his
Son.

The call of God is the call of the bridegroom for his bride, a lover
yearning for consummation of a divine relationship with those he
created, his beloved, who God wills to become the very bride of
Christ.[22] Those who pursue these longings, using the analogies of

John Bunyan, begin at the City of Destruction and pass through the Gate of Salvation, where their burden of sin is removed by the sacrifice of Jesus Christ. Now they embark on a narrow path with few signposts, but with a partial vision of glorious reality at the end. This lifelong journey of discipleship does not end until Christ's return.

Many are motivated to consider this journey because they have observed pilgrims who call themselves Christians and who seem to have found something winsome and powerful. These are pilgrims who have followed Peter's instructions to "always be prepared to give an answer to everyone who asks you to give the reason for the hope that you have. But do this with gentleness and respect, keeping a clear conscience, so that those who speak maliciously against your good behavior in Christ may be ashamed of their slander" (1 Pet 3:15-16).

In this way an invitation is given to come along on the journey and discover the reality of that hope in Jesus. Christ himself has opened this narrow and difficult path. Along the way there will be times of great joy and refreshment. But equally, there will be discouragement, temptations, attacks from evil powers and enticements to satisfy the heart's longings in Vanity Fair, where the world seduces us with its promise of self-fulfillment, power and indulgence.

This spiritual quest, therefore, is a journey from our known present reality to God's hopeful future; following what Jesus called the *narrow way*—the less chosen path that disavows the ways of the world in a heart search for this loving God. On this narrow road there is no distinction between public and private sectors of life. The expectation of Jesus is a stringent one—to disavow self-seeking and to willingly serve him as Lord of all our life.

Along the pathway the pilgrim sheds the vestiges of the old world. The truths of Jesus become internalized as divine reality, not as sterile rules to be obeyed legalistically. In the process, the pilgrim is set free from old ways and, though always human and imperfect, progressively takes on the very character of the Lord himself.

The call of the Great Commission. Christ's Great Commission calls us as we go on this pilgrimage to reach out when led by the Holy Spirit to others as we meet them and point the way forward. No matter how sophisticated our methods and media, there is overwhelming evidence that people come to Christ initially and grow in the Spirit through face-to-face witness and involvement.[23] This pilgrimage, in actuality, is a decision process.

More than twenty-five years ago Engel and Sogaard analyzed the nature of this decision process and its implications for evangelism and discipleship.[24] The so-called Engel scale ("the spiritual decision process") appears in figure 4.2. While some readers will be familiar with this, its relevance for the current practice of world missions warrants our repeating it here.

The concept is a logical one in which God and communicator cooperate as seen in figure 4.1.

Ministry	God's Role	Communicator's Role
Spiritual growth	Sanctification	Follow-up & activation (teaching & discipling)
Rebirth	Regeneration	No role
Evangelism	Conviction	Seed sowing & watering
Making God's existence known	General revelation	No role

Figure 4.1. Cooperation between God and communicator

The scale in figure 4.2 should be read from bottom to top. It shows various stages in the pilgrimage, starting from no background or awareness of the Christian faith, moving through conversion and on into a lifelong pattern of growth and maturity as a Christian. There is no terminal point, of course, because maturity as a disciple is a continuing process, with no point at which one can be said to "have arrived," at least not until we become like Jesus, when we "see him as he is" (1 Jn 3:2).

Everyone is somewhere on this scale, and the challenge is, with a spirit of discernment, to start where they are. But modernity has infected evangelism with a zeal to *motivate* decisions. As a result, evangelism is frequently undergirded by the unrecognized assumption that all nonbelievers are at the stage where they are ready for a change of allegiance, that they recognize a problem in their lives and have a clear and unambiguous desire to do something about it—to enter into a relationship with Jesus. An attempt to motivate this response prematurely can quickly bring about misunderstanding, resentment and even a short-lived, insincere faith.[25]

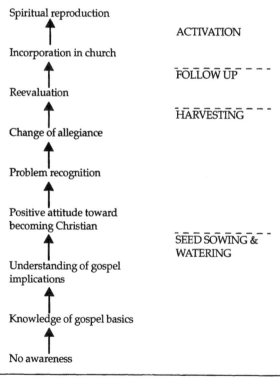

Figure 4.2. The spiritual decision process

The model of a pilgrimage, or journey, envisions conversions differently. Once an initial response to the gospel has taken place, the pilgrim joins other believers as they walk down that narrow way of death to self and new life in Christ. All that is asked of the pilgrim is a desire to know the reality of these life-changing truths. This jour-

ney then is one of progressively learning and grasping more of this
divine truth. And with this comes a progressive, positive change
toward becoming a true believer.

As Jesus' parable of the soils (Mt 13:3-9) makes clear, only a
minority of nonbelievers will respond positively and persevere.
Those who do persevere will be forced to wrestle with the ultimate
meaning of the gospel. Conviction of sin leads to receiving forgiveness and rebirth through Jesus. And when spiritual regeneration has
taken place, the pilgrim hopefully will persevere and grow in grace
through spiritual sanctification. The process of becoming a disciple
is never completed in this life. Conversion is just one, albeit essential, stage in the process, but it is not in and of itself the goal. As we
have stressed repeatedly, *the Great Commission will never be fulfilled
prior to the return of Christ.*

A change of allegiance (conversion) may entail a decision process
lasting a lifetime, or it may occur in the flash of a moment. While
"coming forward" or "praying the sinner's prayer" may prove helpful to some, the act of regeneration is a sovereign work of the Holy
Spirit, not an action inspired by any prescribed tactic. As the apostle
Paul stressed in 1 Corinthians 3, it usually requires multiple influences over a lifetime, no one of which is decisive in and of itself. For
that reason, it is misleading to attribute the number of so-called converts to single-event conversions.

Evangelicals have commonly presumed that the entire world can
be won for Christ. But all Jesus ever asked of his disciples is to harvest where the fields are ripe, leaving the scope and the magnitude
of the outcome entirely to him.

Incorporation into Christian community. The spiritual growth of pilgrims is all but impossible unless we "consider how we may spur
one another on toward love and good deeds." As the author of
Hebrews goes on to say, "Let us not give up meeting together, as
some are in the habit of doing, but let us encourage one another"
(Heb 10:24-25). The new believer must be incorporated into a Christian community.

We have generally avoided using the word *church* up to this
point. As we will argue in the next chapter, existing churches world-

wide are more often characterized by *institutionalization* than by *community*. What this means is that the church all too often has yielded to modernity and has become an institution made up of largely autonomous individuals governed by hierarchy, delegation of authority, formality and ministry through ever-expanding programs.[26]

But the essence of community is *mutual, motivated connectedness,* a concept poorly understood in a culture permeated by modernity and its preferences for autonomous individuality. For community to take place, individuality must yield to accountability and mutuality, to a recognition that the whole thrust of New Testament revelation is directed to a corporate body, in which members minister to each other and to the world under the lordship of Jesus. Its nature, motivation and message sharply contradict the corrupting premises of modernism, which values individualistic autonomy and independence.

Lesslie Newbigin has prophetically observed that Christian community is the hermeneutic of the gospel, its very message and medium.[27] The implications of this are powerful. When the church is institutionalized and drawn in on itself, it has little to say to a world that it so closely mirrors. But true community of transformed believers can be genuine salt and light as common people do uncommon deeds. True Christian community interprets the gospel for the world.

Consider the purpose statement of Saddleback Church in the United States: "To bring people to Jesus and *membership* in his family, develop them to Christ-like *maturity,* and equip them for their *ministry* in the church and life *mission* in the world in order to magnify God's name [italics ours].[28]

Notice the commitment to *unleashing the people of God.* This usually does not take place through passive participation in congregational worship, teaching and programs—as important as these are to the life of any church. God's plan calls for building the body of Christ through spiritually gifted individuals who have been discipled and equipped to follow him individually and corporately both within and beyond the walls of the church. As Vinay Samuel puts it,

"The Holy Spirit through His gifts works through the church to enable the people of God to become salt and light in the wider society, addressing it with values and power of the Kingdom of God in all areas, economic, political, social and religious."[29]

In short, the body is unleashed to express the reign of Christ as its members follow the Spirit's leading. The Beatitudes (Mt 5:3-11) well express the essence of this daily life on kingdom living:

☐ *obedience*—through being humble-minded and without pride, hungering and thirsting after righteousness, and being pure in heart

☐ *manifestation of love*—through showing mercy and being a peacemaker

☐ *nonconformity to the world*—through genuine identification with victims of unrighteousness and through gentleness and total identification with the purposes of God even to the point of suffering and persecution

For all of this to happen in world missions, we can no longer fall prey to planting churches that are little more than carbon copies of their institutionalized counterparts in the West. It is time to come to grips with this essential question: *what is the nature of the churches we are planting?* We will tackle this issue in chapter five.

Following in the steps of the Master. Jesus illustrated vividly how to take others on a spiritual pilgrimage in obedience to his Great Commission. From our discussion so far, it is apparent that he presented the whole gospel to the whole person through a seamless integration of evangelism and social transformation. He rarely launched a dialogue with words. Rather it was his actions and compelling presence that caught the attention of others and authenticated his message. Furthermore, he never deviated from his total dependence on the Holy Spirit. But there are other lessons to be learned from Jesus.

Development of servant leaders. Jesus could have become a charismatic leader who mobilized the multitudes and led the masses to overthrow Roman oppression and establish his kingdom on earth. Certainly he would have attracted any number of obedient followers. But he knew this was not the will of the Father. Instead he exercised a very different kind of leadership—servant leadership dedicated to empowering others who would embody and proclaim the gospel of the reign of God.

Most of his earthly ministry was devoted to instilling the qualities of servant leadership in a handful of disciples who would each play his part in establishing and building a church that survives to this day. The Gospels are filled with practical daily lessons in what it means to disavow power and self-seeking and to serve by putting the consideration of others above all personal concerns. These lessons have survived through the ages and still form the very background of enlightened leadership in all sectors of society.

Leadership development, tragically, has been almost entirely absent in the world missions strategies of this century. This, of course, is yet another damaging extension of the great omission of spiritual formation in prevailing concepts of the Great Commission. The shepherds have not been trained to disciple and equip the flock. We are convinced that leadership development is today's *greatest* priority, and we will have more to say on this subject in the remaining chapters.

Strategic thinking. Jesus was a strategic thinker. He always met others where they were on their pilgrimage. He was a master of using familiar images, illustrations from real life, and effective parables. He wanted to be understood. With this practical approach, he could quickly move a person from what was known and familiar to what was new and challenging. He also was dedicated to speaking to a person's current realities and needs, and to God's working in their life.

When talking with the Samaritan woman (John 4), Jesus started with the need they both shared—to quench their thirst. She could understand just what he meant when he asked for a drink, even though it was unusual for a Jew to talk with a Samaritan, let alone a woman. From that obvious and concrete beginning he quickly moved to the deep spiritual insights she needed. Similarly, Jesus spoke to the felt need of the man at the pool in John 5 as a natural way to get to the heart of the issue. "Do you want to get well?" "Of course I do." "Then pick up your mat and walk."

Jesus had no preconceived tactic that he used in all situations. He said to Nicodemus, "No one can see the kingdom of God unless he is born again" (Jn 3:3). But he did not say that to the woman at the well, the man by the pool or the rich young ruler (Mk 10:17-22) or in any other recorded instance. Nor did Jesus say to Nicodemus, "If you knew the gift of God and who it is that asks you for a drink, you would have asked him and he would have given you living water" (Jn 4:10). Rather than a preconceived strategy he used in all situations, Jesus adapted his strategy to each unique situation, while always remaining true to the biblical pattern of God's dealings with Israel and the world.

Today's preoccupation with methods, we argue, owes more to a modern worldview than it does to these biblical patterns. While methods can be quite useful if used with wisdom, we are disturbed by the unending flood of Western agencies and teachers who are advocating "tried and true methods" worldwide. All too often the unfortunate outcome is captivity to a methodology that is inappropriate to the context. We urge a moratorium on this practice. The time has come for a return to biblically based wisdom that follows our Lord's example of adapting to each context.

Obedience to an eternal timetable. How would Jesus have fit into this era of massive mobilization of missions resources to "finish the work" in a short period of time? In fact, he might seem to be a genuine misfit. How could he let the rich young ruler go without enlisting him to the cause and harnessing his great wealth to advance the kingdom? Why did he spend most of his three-year ministry teaching a very ordinary, unpromising group of disciples at the very time when the fields were ripe for harvest? How could he daily pass by numerous ministry opportunities that might have been leveraged for the kingdom if only he mobilized his followers more intensively and effectively?

We think it is far more likely that he would shun the massive evangelism programs of today and work as he usually did, one person at a time, focusing on those who were ready to hear his message. There is no reason to envision Jesus changing his priorities and timetable in response to the pressures of a new millennium. It is time to put aside our preoccupation with reaching the masses through all viable means as quickly as possible and learn from his example.

Moving Ahead in a Postmodern Era

In this chapter we have advocated a decisive break with the persistent assumptions of modernity that have contaminated world missions for more than a century. It is our contention that we need to return to Christ's mission of establishing and extending his reign. We have envisioned a *kingdom paradigm of world missions* that is (1) sensitive to the initiative of God, (2) motivated by a vision of the reign of Christ, (3) characterized by mutual sharing from multiple centers of influence and (4) committed to partnership and collaboration.

It is helpful once again to reflect on how today's postmoderns differ from their older counterparts. First, and most emphatically, they have come to see the assumptions of modernity with all of its technological and rational superiority, as being largely bankrupt. They are suspicious of dogmatic arguments and propositional claims. But they have restored a sense of faith, albeit a tentative and uncertain faith without a definite direction or end.

They also affirm community and the importance of yielding a blind motivation for self-actualization to something with a higher purpose or goal. They are open to a spiritual journey, an authentic pilgrimage with seekers, believers and nonbelievers, who are still in the process of drawing closer to their Master. They will come along if they see a true Christian faith modeled, first of all, and then proclaimed.

The kingdom paradigm of world missions calls for a return to the model of Jesus, whose life was dedicated to discerning where his Father was at work and joining him in helping those on a spiritual pilgrimage to move closer to their Lord and Savior. This pattern of ministry is as contemporary today as it was in his time: (1) developing servant leaders, (2) thinking strategically, and (3) obeying an eternal timetable.

Bud Anderson and his fellow leaders at GHM, as well as the missions team at First Church of Rollingwood, are at the point where they are ready to break from the past. This too will require a ministry pilgrimage that moves down largely unmarked paths and requires an attitude of risktaking and entrepreneurship that is empowered and motivated by the Holy Spirit. What will this journey look like? Join us in the next chapters as we attempt to shed some light on the steps that lie ahead.

5

....

The Church
in Missions

After a particularly long and frequently boring monthly meeting with most of the other pastors in Rollingwood churches, Pastor Geoff Finch came back into his office exhausted and somewhat disillusioned. Here are just a few of the common frustrations all seemed to be facing:

☐ The youth are not responding to "youth club" type ministries that had been so successful in the past.

☐ The traditional "singles" ministry isn't working in the same way that had seemed to be so cutting edge a decade or so ago.

☐ The need for children's ministries seems to be exploding at the very time volunteer church nursery programs no longer meet the need.

☐ Preaching in effective and compelling ways week by week is becoming increasingly difficult.

☐ Too many come to the church for various activities or for their children but rarely attend Sunday worship.

How could he face the missions committee, which was about to meet? Suddenly he came to an important insight that changed everything—the problems with this program are reflected in many other things First Church is doing. Now he realized what God was showing this committee through these months of biblical study and reflection: the tensions faced in the missions program are really just a symptom of a fundamental misunderstanding of the very nature of the church.

*   *   *

THERE ARE IMPORTANT HISTORICAL AND CULTURAL FACTORS BEhind Pastor Finch's illumination. Not very long ago the church was assumed by everyone to be one of the central institutions of Western culture. The physical location of churches in the center of most American cities testifies to this seminal role. The pastor was automatically considered to be a community leader; he (rarely a "she" in those days) typically was asked to pray before community events, whether the high school homecoming football game or the Fourth of July picnic. There was a widely shared agreement even among nonchurchgoers that "Christian values" were the basis of civilization as it was understood.

Whatever one may think of this situation (and it had its own limitations), the cultural centrality of the church has been undergoing a radical transformation for more than a century. In particular, other "faiths" (especially secularism) now compete with Christianity in the marketplace of ideas. As Craig van Gelder put this recently: "Expectations of privileged position [for Christianity] gave way to irrelevance and marginalization. People no longer assumed that the church had anything relevant to say on matters beyond personal faith. Public policy became increasingly secularized, as public morals became increasingly privatized."[1]

Because of these changes, we find ourselves in a situation in which perceptions about the church have come to constitute a major challenge for pastors and Christian leaders. George Barna discovered in 1993 that the public in all sectors of society was unanimous in the conviction that the local church no longer is sensitive to its needs. Among unchurched people, for example, only 9 percent felt the church had continuing relevance for them (though twice as many believed that Christianity as a religion is still relevant!).[2] This reflects the fact that Americans are more likely to be interested in spiritual matters than they are in the institutional church.

To further underscore the extent of spiritual interests of all shapes and varieties, *Publisher's Weekly* reports that growth in the number of religious book titles has been unprecedented. From 1994 to 1996 these titles increased by 500 percent, increasing by another 40 percent in 1997 and 58 percent by August 1998. Furthermore, the rate of religious book sales through the Internet as reported by Amazon.com is currently outpacing all other areas of interest, including business.[3]

With this exploding interest in religion, why then are the churches, at least in the mainline denominations, experiencing such decline in terms of vitality and interest? George Hunsinger points out one reason for this change. He argues that today's church is the recipient of an often unnoticed heritage from the Reformation.[4] The church for the Reformers, was the "place where certain things happen"—preaching, sacraments, discipline and so on. This was in sharp contrast to the church during the later Middle Ages, which ceased to be a place where the gospel could be heard. Happily, during the Reformation the pulpit became a free space where the gospel could again be heard.[5] The result was that the sermon, and related media such as the broadsheet and woodcuts, became powerful instruments of evangelism during that time.

It is undeniable that the church is no longer conceived by the vast majority as the cultural space where certain critical things happen, even as its institutional shape communicates traditional notions. Indeed postmodernity has drastically undermined a view of culture in which religious faith in general and Christian belief in particular provided the unifying bonds for a coherent worldview. Today, given the pervasiveness of pluralism and the accompanying ethnic and social diversity, this is no longer credible for many people. In fact, no single voice or entity can claim to speak for everyone today. As a result, many traditional structures are under attack, including the institutional church.

It is not hard to see why so many in today's world do not relate to the church as it is currently organized. It appears to be large and bureaucratic in the face of a widespread desire for close and intimate relationships. The often abstract moral codes it offers do not touch the postmoderns' spiritual quest for personal fulfillment. In short, the church is seen to harbor hypocrites rather than genuine strugglers for meaning. A primary characteristic of today's postmodern generation is its suspicion of large, impersonal structures and its longing for community. We see this as a wonderful opportunity for the church and for the missionary life that should characterize this church.

Meanwhile, changing patterns of work and family life—long commutes, weekend soccer practice and games, the proliferation of entertainment options—keep people occupied. It is little wonder churches often fail to connect with people, and pastors like Geoff Finch struggle to make their programs attractive. Yet Geoff along with many others are beginning to sense that renewed interest in the role of faith and religion, especially among the postmodern generation, may provide a new opportunity for Christians to recover a biblical sense of mission. For this to happen, however, the institutional church must come to grips with why its inherited structure is largely unable to cope with today's realities and what must happen for it to become a vital force once again.

Two Contrasting Models of the Church

Two problems currently face the institutional church. On the one hand, the inherited institutional patterns—a place where things happen—do not allow for the flexibility needed to take advantage of the cultural changes; at the other extreme, the very nature of institutionalization often serves to distort the organic nature of the church. Fortunately, current rethinking about the role of the church in contemporary culture provides a unique opportunity for Christians to recover a biblical model of both missions and the church itself. Let us look at these institutional patterns more closely.

The institutional model. The institutional model of the church embodies a formal structure of governance characterized by hierarchy, formality, delegation and ministry through ever expanding programs. The final authority most often rests with a governing board to whom the pastoral staff is accountable, who are designated by such terms as *deacons, elders* or simply as *the board.* Various committees, in turn, are given responsibility for the ministries of the church and are the primary source for program determination and oversight.

When the assumptions underlying this structure are examined closely, the influence of modernity becomes clear. In fact, in certain respects it would appear that today's institutional model is closer to that of the business firm of the 1960s or a governmental institution than it is to the New Testament. By its structure it seems to encourage (1) individuality, (2) program orientation, (3) a preoccupation with numbers, (4) passivity and (5) resistance to change.

1. Individuality. The institutionalized church, with its roots in modernity, places a high premium on individuality. In America, persons attend church for a variety of reasons that have more to do with personal needs and longings than they do with a sense of response and obedience to a holy God. There are contrary signs, of course, such as the burgeoning small-group movement, and these may be an important corrective. But the church often is a far cry from the model outlined in the New Testament and lived out through the Wesleyans, the Moravians and others in church history.

2. Program orientation. Because of its organizational structure the institutional church requires a proliferation of leader-initiated programs to justify its existence. As Jacques Ellul has noted, this reflects the technological mentality of modernity, which embraces efficiency and growth as the ultimate criteria of success.[6] Methods and resources are systematized to attain preestablished results. Therefore, program maintenance quickly becomes a primary goal epitomized by the all-too-common prayer "Lord, please bless what we are going to do."

Our quarrel does not lie with programs per se—they are necessary for any organized social entity to function in a public way. The real problem lies with a top-down leadership style that endeavors, in effect, to mobilize and fit people into these programs and discourages initiatives from within the church family. Such a practice, when taken to extreme, as it often is, effectively inhibits lay initiative and all but emasculates the unique essence of what the body of Christ is intended to be.

3. *A preoccupation with numbers.* Program orientation can become pernicious when it is infused with the Western preoccupation with numerical growth. We are united, of course, in the conviction that numerical growth as a strategic goal has no scriptural foundation whatsoever, for reasons given in earlier chapters. When it is a driving focus, there is a strong tendency to base programs on those activities that attract the most newcomers and produce the greatest retention among existing members. But these numbers are all too often attracted by skillful marketing methods, thus supplanting the slow work of Christian nurturing.

There is no question that churches engage head-to-head in effective competition to attract a church-shopping public. Thus a primary focus is placed on facilities and diversity of programming, which are all-too-frequently undertaken only at the cost of a debilitating accommodation to culture.

Jesus also attracted the masses in his day, but this seemed to cease abruptly at the synagogue in Capernaum after his most pointed reference to his divinity and the necessity to "eat the living bread from heaven" (Jn 6:48-51). The crowd quickly began to turn away in confusion and disillusionment. Jesus knew why this was happening and offered this explanation to his brothers: "The world cannot hate you, but it hates me because *I testify that what it does is evil*" (Jn 7:7, emphasis ours).

Jesus pulled no punches when he stressed the radically countercultural nature of his basic message—"Take up your cross and follow me." As this theme echoed through his ministry after Pentecost, the numbers dwindled radically. This is precisely the outcome the church can expect when it becomes appropriately prophetic, moving beyond its current North American preoccupation with a narrow range of issues such as homosexuality and abortion, and moves to point out the endemic corruption in society that so quickly leads to oppression and injustice.

It should be abundantly clear that Christianity, under most circumstances, is destined to be a minority religion, albeit an amazingly effective one, when its message is properly heard. *Numerical growth, if it occurs at all, is an outcome of the church functioning as a winsome alternative to society under the lordship of Christ. It is not the primary goal!* It is time to end the numerical preoccupation that originated through Western modernity and has swept throughout the entire Christian world.

4. *Passivity.* Another unfortunate consequence of institutionalism is passivity. In the course of our ministry, both of us have interacted with thousands of pastors and Christian leaders worldwide. Often the question is asked, "What percentage of your congregation is active in the Christian life over and above Sunday involvement?" This strikes a painful chord, because the most common answer is 10 percent or less. The only exception is with newly planted churches, where involvement is far higher—at least at the outset.

Do not fail to grasp the implications of this finding. What it says is that the vast majority in the institutional church are passive participants. And who can blame them? By its pattern of control and direction from the top, the atmosphere in which they worship asks little or nothing of them. There is little attempt to unleash lay initiative. Is it any wonder that the church is often shallow and without significant influence on the culture around it?

5. *Resistance to change.* In one sense institutionalism and its program orientation is a reflection of the desire to protect and preserve Christian practices and teaching in the face of almost overwhelming change. There are those in every era who lament the trends around them and call on the church to return to its roots and to avoid letting "the world squeeze us into its own mold." As a result the church often overreacts and adopts a "hunker down" mentality.

All these characteristics result in an inertia that, with the best intentions in the world, can scarcely be overcome. We argue that it is this same inertia and lack of vision that has afflicted the Western missions movement. In both cases the failure is, in an important sense, theological: we do not grasp what God is doing in calling out a pilgrim people who will seek his glory in all of life and throughout all of culture. In both church and missions then, techniques and programs are made to replace a spirit-filled mobilization of every believer.

The church as an organism. Pastor Geoff Finch and many others like him face a twofold challenge. First, they wrestle with structures that are unresponsive and inflexible, and second, they struggle to find those particular spaces in the culture that are uniquely suited to the effective communication of the gospel. If we believe that the gospel is good news for all places and times, and that the risen Christ is ultimately the Lord of history and culture, then we can assume that no place is completely resistant to the announcement and embodiment of the reconciling grace of God. The question that Geoff faces is whether the church can respond to this situation and be all that God has called it to be. Or are its structures so fixed that such response is precluded?

The practice of over-adapting to cultural realities such as modernity certainly is not new in the history of the church. What is important for us today is to learn from the ways the church has dealt with these cultural influences in previous periods. Throughout its history various movements of renewal have emerged that sought to deliver the church from its cultural captivity. In the early church and Middle Ages, monastic movements and new religious orders sought to return the church to its original mission; later the Reformation, Pietism and revivalism offered their own critiques of cultural practices that were inimical to the gospel.

Notice that in every case these movements, while resisting certain cultural trends, made selective use of other cultural opportunities to organize themselves and present the gospel. In the earliest church the apostles made ready use of the infrastructure of the Roman Empire—its roads and transportation systems as well as its urban environment—to spread the gospel and to challenge the universal claims of the emperor. This accommodation would have been impossible a few centuries earlier.

During the Middle Ages the monasteries became repositories of culture and centers of learning when no cultural provision was being made around them for these critical activities. And as we have already noted, the Reformers made use of the central place of the church of that period to preach the gospel with a new freedom. Finally, the pietism and revivalism of more recent times capitalized on a turn inward toward personal reflection and (more recently) developing technologies, to give people space to discover the freedom that the gospel allows.

Today in an important sense both the church and missions structures have been influenced by the values and structures of modernity. They both stand in need of new patterns of relationship that will allow the Holy Spirit to renew their sense of missions while they make selective and wise use of the surrounding cultural influences.

We argue that the institutionalized form of the church has distorted its own nature as the living body of Christ in the world and become inflexible. In reality the church, when it is most alive and vital, functions as a creative influence on the culture. It is more like a living and responsive *organism* than an *organization*. When the church leads by means of its institutional face and its highly bureaucratic structures, on the other hand, it risks losing touch with the world it is meant to serve. Far more seriously, though, it risks losing its biblical identity as the spiritual and visible body of Christ. This identity is rooted in certain theological realities that are not optional or subject to negotiation: (1) its nature as a living temple for God, (2) its ministry through gifts of the Spirit, (3) its nature as a society of mutual love and service, (4) its servant leadership, (5) its community, and (6) its outward focus.

1. A living temple. The church as the people of God finds its identity, strength and mandate in the reality of the trinitarian God. Christ died to redeem the people, and by the Holy Spirit they are made into a living temple for God. Because of Christ's death, resurrection and ascension God has "placed all things under his feet and appointed him to be head over everything for the church, which is his body, the fullness of him who fills everything in every way" (Eph 1:22-23). Thus the people of God are constituted and empowered by the indwelling presence of Christ by the Spirit. Their unity and their witness grow out of and reflect this presence in the world.

Now there is a tendency to think that these ideas are abstract and without significance for how we operate our organizations. But for Paul nothing could be further from the truth. He lived in a day in which various forms of Greek philosophy and practice competed with each other and multiple forms of social organizations and religious faiths struggled to be heard. In this context, he sought uncompromisingly to work from carefully defined theological premises. Equally importantly, as his epistles make clear, he sought to work out ways they all could live together as Christians that would reflect, indeed embody, these theological realities. The presence of God through the Spirit, the lordship of Christ, the good news of the gospel—these were the operative realities to which he sought to adapt the emerging communities.

2. *Ministry through gifts of the Spirit.* The ministry that the church offers the world follows from these theological foundations and reflects the gifts that the Spirit has distributed in tribute to the work of Christ. Ephesians 4 argues that "to each one of us grace has been given as Christ apportioned it" (v. 7). This means that everyone in the body, by virtue of his or her baptism, has received grace that reflects Christ's mighty work. Moreover, as the succeeding verses argue, this giftedness—apostles, evangelists, teachers or whatever—is for the sake of the building up of the body, until it reaches maturity, "the fullness of Christ" (vv. 11-13).

The central task of the church as a living organism is, as we stressed in chapter four, to *unleash the gifted people of God to extend his reign through the whole world.* What this means is that the church is meant to lead and minister through its giftedness. As it has been graced by Christ through the Spirit, so it is meant to go into the world as the aroma and agent of God. This is not to say that regular planning and reflection are unnecessary, but, these are to be disciplined and ordered by the leading of the Spirit and pursued in constant prayer.

What a contrast this is to a church where programs are determined by leaders with little or no corporate input and "sold" to the body through multiple forms of persuasion. Nowhere in the New Testament is the stress in ministry laid on one group of people to the exclusion of another. Indeed in Acts no sooner are certain people set aside to wait tables (in Acts 6) than they begin to preach and teach the word to any who come in their path. We can well understand why Geoff Finch is disturbed about the dwindling impact of the programs at First Church. It is entirely possible that these programmatic efforts have little to do with the full power of the leadership of the Spirit.

3. *A society of mutual love and service.* The common distinction between pastor and laity is specious, because the word "laity" embraces the entirety of the people of God. In fact in 1 Corinthians 12 Paul goes out of his way to argue that those whose gifts may seem insignificant in the body, may in fact have the greater honor (1 Cor 12:20-23). In all cases, based on the gifts given by the Spirit, everyone has a role to play, until all members come to maturity in Christ. Moreover the church is to be characterized by a mutual loving service, both toward those inside and outside the church. It appears that mutual burden bearing became a kind of shorthand for the moral demands that Christianity placed on its early members (see Gal 6:2).

4. *Servant leadership.* The role of leadership in the organic church takes the form of motivation and empowerment. This is in sharp contrast to the *big boss* model, which is prevalent in much of the world, whereby leaders initiate and control most of what happens in and through the organization. Jesus exhibited a radically different servanthood model designed to produce mature, gifted disciples and to release them to take initiative to be salt and light in his kingdom reign. The goal, as we have said before, is to unleash the potential of the body of Christ, not to recruit their participation in programs designed by someone else.

5. *Community.* The purpose of this universal giftedness and valuation in the sight of God, Paul goes on to say, is so that there may be no dissension in the body but rather a mutual caring for one another. This is the very essence of Christian community—*motivated connectedness.* It is small wonder that loving care for one another, the primary evidence of the spiritual ministry of the church, proved to be such a powerful witness in the early church.[7]

6. *An outward focus*. The final implication of this theological structure is the world directedness of the body of Christ. In the famous high priestly prayer of John 17, Jesus says, "As you sent me into the world, I have sent them into the world" (v. 18). The whole direction of God's work is toward embodying his glory in the world, from creation through to the new creation. As C. S. Lewis put it:

> Creation seems to be delegation through and through. [God] will do nothing simply of himself which can be done by creatures. I suppose this is because he is a giver. And has nothing to give but himself. And to give himself is to do his deeds—in a sense, and on varying levels to be himself—through the things he has made.[8]

Therefore, God's people empowered by the Spirit are continuing the great work of Christ, which was not only to take God into the world but to bring the world to God.

Can These Institutionalized Bones Live?
We believe that these institutionalized bones can live, but it will require a substantial effort to recapture the organic nature of the church.[9] Churches that have made this attempt demonstrate important commonalities:

☐ a conviction that numerical growth, if it occurs at all, is a spontaneous outcome motivated by the Holy Spirit rather than a goal

☐ a commitment to intentional spiritual formation with particular focus on discovery and use of spiritual gifts in a manner consistent with the mission of Jesus as expressed in Luke 4:18-21

☐ a consistent church identity based on the distinctly countercultural message of Jesus expressed through prophecy and radical love for those who are persecuted and oppressed

☐ a genuine commitment to servant leadership characterized by Christian vision and empowerment

☐ a concept of church programming and ministry built around encouraging lay initiative, with church programs limited primarily to facilitating an unleashed laity

☐ an expectation that vital discipleship requires the accountability, encouragement and support that can only take place through community, expressed in the form of small cells throughout the church

☐ an unwavering commitment to mobilizing the entire body of Christ to fulfill Christ's mandate to make disciples first in one's Jerusalem, then in Judea and finally in the entire world

☐ a disavowal of modernity's shaping influence on Christian missions, accompanied by a commitment to follow the New Testament model for the ministry as it is adapted to a contemporary world

If steps such as these are undertaken following the leadership of the Holy Spirit, then and only then will world missions once again become a vital reality. As we have been arguing throughout, the body of Christ is not something secondary to missions but is the very heart and core of that activity. The church is itself the primary message and the medium of God's presence in the world, though God's activity of course is not limited to that body. The church exists by mission, in Emil Brunner's famous expression, as fire exists by burning.

World Missions in a Revitalized Local Church

Missions activity is that particular work of crossing cultural and philosophical barriers to embody and announce the love of God as seen in Jesus Christ. The fundamental reality is that these common activities define the very identity and meaning of the church as a reflection of the trinitarian character of God. This means that missions cannot be simply another program in the life of the church, competing for always-limited financial resources. Rather missions is the reason for which all other ministries exist.

Bruce Camp has observed that churches fall into three differing categories with respect to their commitment to world missions:

1. *Supporting:* a passive form of involvement characterized by a church/missions-agency relationship in which the church plays a passive role of providing candidates, funds and prayer (a pass-through relationship). The primary initiative here lies with the agency. This model is still prevalent, although it is beginning to diminish.

2. *Sending:* a policy shifting from pass-through relationships, with the church initiating and owning the process of motivating and

sending missionaries. Now the church takes initiative quite apart from those of outside entities and will increasingly look askance upon those who view the church only as the source of funds and candidates.

3. *Proactive (synergistic):* a proactive commitment whereby the church mobilizes its resources and takes initiative to accomplish a specific task in missions often in partnership with agencies and other entities. This is a move far beyond sending in that the church now is pursuing its own strategies throughout the world.

If the church is understood as the community of God's people whose life is defined by mission, it is clear why churches cannot be seen simply as a pass-through for money and personnel as they traditionally have been. This became common practice in an era when churches were remote from the world beyond their borders because of technological limitations in both mobility and communication. It was virtually impossible, for example, for a church in Rollingwood one hundred years ago to even conceive of a hands-on ministry elsewhere in the world.

Therefore, both denominational and independent agencies came into existence and provided a valid and significant way for an isolated church to extend itself meaningfully to the world. Unfortunately, one of the lingering effects of the structure of missions created in an earlier day is the attitude on the part of many missions executives and missionaries that the churches are simply the source of resources—money and personnel, or perhaps gifts in kind. The outcome, of course, is that the full identity and power of the body of Christ is underutilized, and the work of Christ in the world ultimately suffers.

We believe that the third paradigm embracing full proactivity offers the best scenario for the reason that the church now takes its rightful role in the kingdom of God. It is grounded in commitment to strategic use of church resources following biblical priorities. This means that missions moves well beyond its all-too-common existence as simply another program in the life of the church. Rather missions—or better yet, the world-embracing, reconciling work of God—becomes the guiding hand on all the church's programs.

Missions in a New Millennium

What can we say concretely about the shape that missions should take given the current cultural perceptions of the church and our biblical mandates? As Geoff Finch reflected on what was beginning to happen in his church, he found himself growing more and more excited about the possibilities for the future. He realized that much of his culture's difficulty with the church (and his problems with the structure of missions!) reflected institutional patterns that had ceased to be effective.

Moreover his reflection on biblical patterns of ministry along with members of the missions committee and GHM staff gave him a whole new sense of direction. To consider what this might mean he spent a great deal of time consulting with trusted colleagues and with missionaries he knew were in touch with current issues. He shared with them his misgivings about the way missions had come to be understood and his new take on the missionary structure of the church. To his surprise he found a consensus emerging about some practical guidelines, as well as some basic principles, that grow out the biblical narrative.

Start with a proper biblical vision of the Great Commission of Jesus Christ. The missions committee at First Church has already taken the first step toward rediscovering what missions should be in the local church through the serious biblical and theological homework they had done over the previous months. The members, including Pastor Geoff, now have more clarity about the Great Commission as given by Jesus and what it means in practical terms. They came to understand that God gave his Son to bring wholeness and healing to the brokenhearted and oppressed, and that it is the work of First Church to proclaim the liberating truth of Jesus through its ministries and corporate life—in the form of an unleashed laity.

The committee spent considerable time formulating a new vision statement built on the principles discussed above. They were greatly helped by correspondence with other churches who were coming to grips with the new paradigm of world mission. They were especially impressed by one purpose statement which declared that the missions committee is "committed to *fostering an en-*

vironment in which sacrifice to a needy world proceeds out of an aware and grateful heart."[10] It was adopted in slightly modified form with little hesitation.

Next, they affirmed that this vision is accomplished through "sending, equipping and creatively supporting those who are specially gifted, trained and called." Furthermore, there was explicit recognition that this is done, wherever possible, through "Paul-Barnabas" partnerships with like-minded mission agencies and Two-Thirds World counterparts. As a result First Church now has a firm platform upon which to build an exciting, contemporary and relevant program of crosscultural outreach.

Adopt a missions perspective within the broader history of the church and its mission. The committee at First Church of Rollingwood soon learned that most of the problems they were encountering were not unique to them—the challenges were similar to those faced in other places and times. It became clear that there was much to learn from others who had passed this way before. This insight came to Pastor Finch when the church sent him to a special Doctor of Ministry seminar on the global mission of the church. It was an eye-opening experience for him, and he shared excitedly with the committee what he learned when he returned.

Geoff's new insights led the committee to modify the emerging missions program in an important way—development of leaders became a primary consideration in all phases of the missions program. As a result the leader of the after-school tutoring program was sent to an evening class on educational reform, and soon she was pursuing an M.A. in the field. The lay director of the short-term missions emphasis attended a seminar on the topic at a nearby school of world mission. Two scholarships were raised for members who wanted to pursue a degree in missions and micro-enterprise development, an emerging program area for the congregation.

Consistently communicate missions vision as a central priority. Surveys of churches with active missions programs always point to one factor, which above all others, guarantees either success or failure—*support and ownership by the pastor.* If this priority is not affirmed on a consistent basis, missions will be just another program, no matter what a missions committee does, and it will be the first to be cut financially. The conclusion is unmistakable—if the pastor and supporting staff are not on board, world missions as a vital force within the church is probably doomed.

It is our experience that most biblically based pastors are aware that God is a missionary God. But they also are tugged and pulled in countless directions by other urgencies, some of which are compelling. Furthermore, there is a constant struggle even in today's most solidly evangelical churches to overcome the pluralistic heresy that Christianity is just one of many equally valid ways to discover God. What this says is that a restoration of missions vision can be an uphill struggle. There simply is no way to avoid this reality.

Often pastoral support becomes intensified and focused, however, through short-term exposure to missions realities. As important as this can be, such a step must be taken with care. The primary requirement is for pastors (or anyone else from the church for that matter) to go as pilgrims who are seeking the voice of the Lord rather than as Western dignitaries. Only rarely, for example, should they go as a teaching or speaking resource.

Furthermore, every attempt should be made to bring about meaningful and "no holds barred" interaction with responsible national leaders who are not seeking Western resources and will "tell it as it is." Often the outcome can be electrifying. Nothing is more powerful than a pastor who becomes a champion for a cause out of burning vision and personal conviction, and who also understands the central role that a Spirit-gifted laity must play.

The best way to raise congregational vision, in turn, is also through participation in short-term missions efforts. Nothing speaks more clearly than firsthand exposure and hands-on involvement. Those who participate and return must be mobilized as participants in the cause of world missions. This is the seedbed out of which lay initiative can emerge.

Undertake a comprehensive evaluation of the existing missions program. Once vision is clarified, the next step is to examine all current missions efforts against these new standards. The goal is to discover as precisely as possible the actual outcomes of the ministry of supported individuals. This, of course, requires interaction with missionaries and their agency executives. Fortunately this is now an accepted practice. When it is done with empathy and understanding, a basis is often laid for constructive partnership.

Individual missionaries. At some point it is almost inevitable that some currently supported individuals should be sensitively and lovingly phased out over time. Clearly such decisions are extremely difficult. Nonetheless there often is no choice for those who have chosen to follow Christ in today's environment rather than following outdated patterns.

When such a step is taken, it must be done in full recognition that a large percentage of today's missionaries went to the field in good faith and in very different times. Tragically, far too many are victim of the pervasive failure of missions boards to develop and equip all missionaries to cope responsively with change, which is a virtual necessity in today's world. The outcome is that a large number of responsible servants of God are faced with the midlife reality of growing irrelevance, in spite of obvious commitment and even competence in areas that are no longer needed.

Although some downsizing is almost inevitable, this must be done in such a way that those who are affected are honored and, where feasible, helped to undergo training and assume new roles. Both the church and the agency have a God-given responsibility to provide a safety net of love and ongoing support.

Missions agencies. The other beam of this searchlight focuses on the agencies themselves. Churches are obligated to carry out responsible reviews of agencies with which they have been connected. We provided a number of standards in the previous chapter that define missions work in today's environment and go far beyond the "bigness is a sign of greatness" mentality so prevalent today. These standards should be used in full expectation that a responsible agency will reply forthrightly without taking offense.

The objective is to gain a clear understanding of ministry outcomes. The most likely response will be a description in numerical terms of what was done—distribution of evangelistic media, attendance at evangelistic meetings and training programs, relief and welfare activities, and so on. Tragically, only a limited few will be able to document sustained outcomes over time in the lives of individuals, a community and a whole nation. Fortunately there are ministry evaluation tools available to assist agencies in this kind of assessment. Ask the agency which of these they regularly employ. If they cannot answer such requests easily, it may be a sign that the agency is working in old paradigms and that partnership may become problematic.

It is understandable that many who adopt a proactive, local church paradigm will tend to look askance at agencies that do not seem to walk to the same drum. It is dangerous practice, however, to write them off in a cavalier manner. These agencies too find themselves faced with changing paradigms, and most of them, in our experience, evidence the very same spirit as Bud Anderson and his leadership team at Global Harvest Mission: they are anxious to follow the Lord and are struggling to find the way.

Consider the realities Bud must face. Over 50 percent of his missionary staff went to the field more than twenty years ago. While most have been diligent to keep up in the limited time they have, they too are blindsided by the diminished and radically changing role for Western missionaries. A particular burden to Bud is to turn over a total of eleven hospitals and orphanages to the local church on seven fields. How well is the local church prepared to assume this big financial and managerial responsibility? Quite frankly, there are no easy answers.

To compound the situation, few missions executives were prepared for the rapidity of the shift from the pass-through paradigm to proactive local church missions initiative. Now they suddenly are faced with a desire within many churches to partner in new ways. Many churches, in fact, are asking for training and help as they take these new steps. Frankly, agencies often are no more prepared than local churches to face these realities and may appear threatened by an aggressive church program. We are in an era without a clear roadmap, going down an all-new highway that we must traverse together.

Finally, almost everyone, both local church and missions leaders, have found themselves unprepared for the dramatic inward turn of churches in the Western world. The outcome is a sharp and unrelenting decline in local church financial support to the point where the survival of many agencies is at stake.[11]

We urge as strongly as possible that local churches continue to financially support those agencies who are turning their face toward change, which we shall explore more in the next chapter. Failure to do so may result in the cause of world missions being crippled prematurely and in an unnecessary manner.

Avoid the temptation to become yet another missions board. The missions committee at First Church of Rollingwood soon understood that while it needed to become more proactive in missions, it should not become simply another missions board in its own right. There is a real danger that churches with a rich diversity of resources can become totally disillusioned with the traditional missions structure and the passive role of the church. At that point it is very tempting to move away from what we have referred to as Mission, Inc., and establish their own missions board, functioning largely independently from existing agencies (and other churches!). We are sympathetic with all who are facing this enticing temptation and recognize the frustration that makes it appear to be a necessity. Nevertheless, we urge those who have not yielded to the temptation to count the costs.

Today's professional missionaries and their boards are in the fortunate position of having learned from both the strengths and the weaknesses of past generations. The changes that have taken place in missions outlook and practice, especially since the end of World War II, are nothing short of astonishing. Most missions have profited from this experience. Make no mistake about it, a retreat from continued agency/church partnership, no matter how well motivated, virtually guarantees that an independent initiative will face the same challenges and make the same mistakes—without the benefit of the experience missions have acquired.

We are concerned that many of the churches building their own independent missions presence reflect a confidence bordering on arrogance that they can "go it alone" without consultation and collaboration with those who have preceded them. When this is undertaken with seemingly unlimited financial backing, the effects can be catastrophic. The fact that they are well-meaning does not justify the harm that a policy of noncooperation can inflict, when the church and agencies could be working together in increasingly productive ways.

Having said this to the churches, we have similar counsel for existing agencies that are tempted to find multiple ways of discouraging the newly emerging local church presence in missions. It is time for a spirit of cooperation and collaboration regardless of past history and existing biases.

Adopt a policy of constructive partnerships with like-minded agencies and entities. Fortunately the missions committee at First Church has chosen not to withdraw support from responsible missionaries and agencies. They recognized that God's calling of longer-term missionaries serving as church planters or evangelists is as critical as it ever was. But this policy was also developed in full awareness that First Church should also launch and support its own initiatives where appropriate, occasionally alone, usually in partnership with GHM or other groups demonstrating a comparable spirit of change.

Given today's realities it is clear that much that is done in missions must be specific, limited and targeted. A church in Africa needs help in lay leadership training; a church association in the Philippines calls for assistance in evangelism; a Central American church association wants help in rebuilding after a devastating hurricane. The need is frequently for short-term efforts, which many local churches are in the ideal position to provide.

On a case-by-case basis, churches need to explore partnerships that complement the gifts and vision of the congregation and further its goals. At times this may be with traditional missions or denominational missions structures, especially when entering areas where the latter have a long history and experience. At other times, partnerships might be undertaken with newer, single-purpose missions or with national missions boards in the Two-Thirds World. The key is to assure that the partnership is strategic, targeted and limited to achievable goals.

In the final analysis, partnerships and alliances affirm the eternal truth that no group in the body of Christ has a monopoly either of vision or gifts. We share and work together, Paul reminds us, "until we all reach unity in the faith and in the knowledge of the Son of God and become mature, attaining to the whole measure of the fullness of Christ" (Eph 4:13). Therefore, local churches and missions agencies need each other, although the priority must always reside with the former.

View world missions as an extension of local presence. Geoff Finch and the committee came to a deeper understanding of the principle that someone who has not proven to be an effective minister and communicator at home most likely would not suddenly become an effective missionary overseas. Furthermore, Geoff also knew that even the best seminary or graduate school missions-training program can rarely make people into effective missionaries by itself.

This principle, however, goes well beyond individual missions candidates, it applies to the church as well. Sally Calderone put it well, after a missions committee meeting a few weeks later, when she stated forthrightly that the missions program at First Church will only be as strong as its local missionary presence. "If little noticeable impact is being made at the neighborhood level," she observed, "what contribution can we expect to take overseas except to continue doling out our funds and providing missionary candidates?"

This group began to see that there was a logical progression in the growing maturity of a congregation's ministry. First, members of the congregation should be encouraged to become actively involved in local projects that are contextualized and effective. Ideally, the congregation could get behind projects that grow out of the vision of various groups in the membership in response to local needs. Or they might get behind the programs proposed by those in the congregation with particular (or professional) expertise in specialized ministries such as doctors in health programs, lawyers in legal aid support and so on.

Further discussion with other members of the church made it apparent that prayer and support could be much more easily mobilized for projects that people had the chance to visit and where they could volunteer. A corollary of this principle, they discovered, is that the impact on the congregation was closely related to the depth and breadth of involvement—both in terms of numbers and of age groups. Actually, this became quite apparent just a few months earlier when there was little interest among those over the age of sixty-five in financially supporting a summer missions project of the college group to Honduras.

These insights led before long to a synergism with the localized ministries in First Church that had never existed before. Previously, it often seemed that each lived in a separate armed camp that fought each other vigorously for funds. Major changes took place when they began to work cooperatively in several programmatic areas. The surprising outcome was that both began to attract volunteers and thrive as never before. Synergism of this type does not happen easily, however, in today's competitive program environment. What it requires is leaders who view the whole world through the eyes of Christ and adopt the conviction that the ministry to Jerusalem and the rest of the world cannot be segmented.

Encourage lay initiative. The missions committee traditionally saw its role as a liaison between the church and agencies. It functioned diligently in a pass-through role, and the result has been a strong missions presence on the field. It rarely occurred to the committee that the church itself could also be an active field participant in the world. An all-new spark was ignited when the youngest member of this committee, Brad Overstreet, began to share what happened to him two years earlier when he was a student at a nearby Christian college.

A number of members of the senior class, including some who are members of First Church, moved into an inner-city apartment complex and began to minister to AIDS-infected mothers and children. As Brad shared their experience, he became more and more excited about the possibility of this small group in the church partnering with an identical ministry he heard about over the Internet in Kampala, Uganda, a country in which most of an entire generation has been ravaged by AIDS. Brad went on to say that he and the others had gained some valuable hands-on experience that could be helpful anywhere in the world. In fact, he volunteered to head up a team to study the possibility of a First Church ministry to AIDS victims that has local roots and extends to the world.

Now the committee was at an interesting crossroads. It is quite probable that a suggestion like this would have been vetoed a decade earlier, when First Church was still mired in the pass-through paradigm. But such was not the case that night. Geoff's new ministerial associate, Ellen Longwood, was the very first to say that this is exactly what the church needs to stimulate fresh, new vision. She and others grasped the advantage of two-way learning and the wonderful possibilities of personnel exchange and networks with others who are expert in this type of ministry.

To the surprise of some veteran committee members, the church board gave quick approval to the proposal and provided enough seed money for three members of the church to become involved with the local ministry Brad mentioned and to visit Kampala at the earliest opportunity. And so a dynamic outreach began to take root from lay initiative. With the nurture and support of this enlightened missions committee, it should flourish over time.

At the same time they were observing an important movement among the under-twenty-five age group who had been on a number of short-term projects together. Geoff noticed their interest in missions had been growing as they spent time traveling and ministering in various places together. During one missions committee meeting they realized that there was a fascinating convergence of postmodern and Christian values taking place under their very eyes. The hunger for genuine community that is so important to postmoderns was being nurtured as they traveled, lived and ministered together. Indeed, missions had become a part of their communal spiritual growth as they went and shared, and more importantly, learned from Christians from various parts of the world. What was happening, Geoff realized, was that missions for this group had become a natural extension of their Christian lifestyle.

View missions as bringing and sending. Today's world is interconnected with the result that missions has become far more than the transmission of resources from here to there—from the center to the periphery. There is a healthy reciprocal emphasis emerging on "bringing."[12] This was to come home to First Church in an unexpected way.

To the surprise of some, Doug Fraser, a retired attorney and member of the missions committee for nearly thirty years, said that he and his wife, Marge, would love to host a return visit to Rollingwood from the leaders of the Kampala outreach. He went on to say, "I think it is about time that we start learning from people like this what missions really is all about in today's world." These prophetic words struck home.

Maintain a spirit of flexibility. It is essential to be sensitive to the leading of the Spirit and flexible to changing cultural (and political) dynamics. An example of this necessity surfaced at First Church in the form of an urgent need to rethink a neighborhood feeding and job development program in the light of the recent welfare reform legislation. Thus it was apparent that a major new avenue of ministry was about to open when government welfare efforts were sharply curtailed by law. The number of homeless people increased within a matter of weeks.

Soon a task force was formed that included, among others, a returned missionary from Africa with a great deal of urban ministry experience and a student from Singapore studying in a local college. The outcome was a recommendation that resulted in a total reorganization of neighborhood social ministries. This might not have happened if the walls of the church were kept tightly closed to world need.

A Restored World Missions Focus

The story we have presented at First Church is hypothetical, of course. Nevertheless, it is an accurate depiction of what must take place to restore a world missions focus within a vital church. You have been given a flavor of what can happen once the church breaks out of its institutional chains and allows the reality of God as a missionary God to strike home. Obviously there is no definitive formula to follow other than simply to *begin to follow the Lord where you are.*

Notice carefully what we have been describing. A fresh vision for missions has grown out of a renewed understanding of what God has called the local church to be and to do. Just as the problems of the one infect the other—indeed they have common sources, as we have seen—so a fresh vision of the body enlivens the sense of missions to the whole world. Recent research has shown that recovery of the dynamic reality of the body of Christ, often experienced in small cell groups within larger congregations, invariably leads to more vital worship and greater outreach.[13] Churches like this are in fact springing up throughout the world (we will describe two below).

The leadership of First Church became convinced that changes like this will continue, even increase, in the days and years ahead. And they saw the need to remain flexible and alert to respond to the challenges as their gifts and talents allow and as the Holy Spirit leads. Geoff Finch and his colleagues realized that ministry is never easy and that the forces of evil continue to oppose the extension of Christ's kingdom. But as he watched AIDS-infected children playing in the churchyard through the newly launched after-school program, he was also aware that the same thing was taking place in Kampala as part of this church. Not surprisingly, Geoff felt a chill of excitement as he grasped the reality of the mutual sharing of gifts worldwide.

Two Case Histories
While the Rollingwood Church is purely hypothetical, we do not want to leave the reader with the impression that nothing like this is really possible. We want to close this chapter with two case studies of actual churches that have realized to a great extent the principles we have outlined in this study. These churches have given us permission to use them as a case study of missions that is collaborative and yet based in the local church. These examples have a great deal to teach us.

Nairobi Chapel. The first case study is from a large city church in Nairobi, Kenya, called Nairobi Chapel. About eight years ago a new seminary graduate, Oscar Muriu, was asked to take over a small struggling chapel near the campus of Nairobi University. Gradually, a ministry developed that focused on raising up leadership from the congregation to take initiative in the outreach ministries of the church, both evangelistic and social. Soon the church had established ambitious goals of having twenty to thirty of their members in active ministry within ten years—you will see that they have raised those goals dramatically. Now daughter churches and health clinics have been established in several poor areas of Nairobi, all staffed by members of Nairobi Chapel. Meanwhile, the small chapel is literally bursting at the seams with three large Sunday services, soon to be increased as you will see, and a full array of weekday training opportunities and outreach programs. To give you a flavor of their vision, we reprint excerpts from a letter Pastor Oscar Muriu wrote recently to his staff and friends. So here is an expression of their missions model in the pastor's own words—notice especially the emphasis on lay initiative, a partnership that stretches literally around the world, and an emphasis on growth that includes a great deal more than numbers alone:

Greetings in that matchless name of our Lord Jesus! This has been a good week for me, and I have been riding on cloud nine! Five people this week have come forward and told me that they have made a decision to go into full-time ministry! Three of these are resigning stable jobs to do so, some are graduates changing their life plans, and one is a single mother (widow) with two children who holds a Masters in Land Economics but feels called into children's ministry. I wish I could tell you about all the exciting things that are happening here! Last week during the worship time, Bob K. led us in a worship/ prayer time when he asked anyone who was feeling down or burdened to put up their hand, and the elders and pastors would surround them and pray—right in the midst of the worship. I was able to pray with a young lady who, as soon as I began, burst out into deep, heart-wrenching sobs. She told me that the man she was going to marry died in a car accident two weeks before, and she was on the verge of committing suicide. After the service I counseled with her, and she accepted the Lord. Two of our pastors' wives know her and are following her up!

This week I also got an e-mail from a member asking if, during my preaching trip to Australia, I could look for translation equipment for our church—we have some fifteen or so mainland Chinese attendees who speak no English but come to the chapel because they enjoy the services. We discovered this ministry last year when Omar [one of the pastors] offered to study the gospel with one if she could find a translator. She did, but Tibaga, who writes our bulletin articles, mistook Omar's request for prayer as an invitation for anyone who speaks Chinese to join a Bible study "he was starting," and advertised it in the bulletin. Eight other Chinese who don't speak English applied! Now they attend the service, and afterwards their translator tells them what all the animation and excitement was about, and also summarizes the sermon! Amazing!

Recently [in] chapel I have been preaching on the vision goals that [were established] during our December elders' retreat. I will give you a summary of them. First—*grow the chapel to its maximum capacity.* We intend to continue growing as though there is nothing else! Last Sunday we probably had as many people sitting outside in our 10 a.m. service as we had inside, and another half sitting outside in the 12:00 service. The 8:15 service is now full up, and this Sunday we expect that there will be people sitting outside. We cannot explain the growth, except that God is at work! Well, we have decided to take it all in and to even encourage numerical growth as the Lord will give it to us. Starting the first Sunday of Feb., we will begin two new services (at Sat. 5:00 and Sun. 5:00). Within a month or two of that we hope to start a "Teens Only" Sun. 2:30 service—what will be a really hip-hop service (I'm still trying to figure out how to preach a message in "Rap"). If the Lord gives additional growth, we will then work at having five Sunday services, five Saturday services, a Friday evening service and a Thursday evening service—twelve in total!

But even that's only the beginning. We have decided to actively become engaged in the political process in Kenya by standing up to address the nation on important matters and being a voice of conscience and commendation as the situation dictates. We are going to begin looking for a hearing with the media (TV, radio and papers—especially seeing that we have people from all three sectors in our congregation). Here it appears the Lord has a humorous way of going before us in this! This last Saturday our name was actually in the papers—rather dubiously in the "Madd" comic strip. The cartoonist had a comment or two (not in negative light thankfully) to say about our toilets! How's that for our "debut" into the media! Anyway, amazingly Kenya Television Network (KTN) called us this week to ask if they could come on Sunday and interview and film the chapel to try and explain why so many Nairobi youth are attending church.

In the meantime, last Sunday one of our church members arranged for me to meet with a British M.P. (conservative), Hon. Gary Streeter, who was in Kenya for a brief working visit. He is a believer and has a passion to see Christian politicians in Parliament in England (a passion we share for our own country). After our discussion I decided to trust God for five members of our congregation to join Parliament at the next elections (by 2002), and for us to begin praying with them now and building believer support teams around them.

Second, we have also committed to another of our dreams: *grow our internship, especially with intention of developing church planters/pastors.* This year we have nine interns (and three recent applications), but we want to believe the Lord to grow these to twenty—thirty per year. For a long time now I have had a vision to begin a "Tyrannus Hall Institute"—a church-based lay development institute preparing people to stand firm as believers in politics, ministry and business, and also conducting an evening Bible school for Nairobi. We have invited a former member of our congregation, who is currently serving as a missionary outside Kenya, to consider coming back to birth this vision after her term outside ends. [He then speaks of an upcoming visit to the U.S. and Australia where some of the pastoral team will study outreach programs of American congregations.]

As preparation for that trip, this year we have challenged the worship teams to construct four musical, evangelistic outreach events each, to write new songs and to each produce a tape or CD for the local market. They are also each to target one of Kenya's neighboring countries and go on a missions trip to minister! Next year (AD 2000), each of the three teams will seek to go outside our continent.

Third, *we plan to decentralize our ministry.* This means going to a localized expression of the meta-church—something that works for us. The idea is that the city is now divided into four districts, each with a full-time pastor, and district elders, who will be responsible to do all the shepherding. The chapel building will become a celebration center for Sundays, without any attempt to "pastor" people there. During the week the main focus will be on leadership development (esp. for church planting), materials, children's and youth ministries, and the construction of well thought-out, "powerful" Sunday services. Baptisms, communion, child dedications, counseling, weddings, burials, etc., will all be conducted by the district leaders.

Fourth, *we plan to start aggressively planting churches.* This year Steve M. [an associate pastor] will start and plant one church. We have also started planting a new church in another poor area (we are working at starting a new clinic with this new church, in addition to our main clinic with its three full-time nurses and which is fully self-financing). We will plant churches using two models: churches planted through our "districts" by relocating members to form the core of a new congregation; and churches planted through "Antioch Teams," people who will go to unreached parts of Nairobi (where we have no members), or relocate to other towns in Kenya, Uganda and Tanzania and plant churches there—churches that fit the context but that seek to embrace what we see as biblical distinctives evidenced at the chapel. Our intention in the next few years is to speed up our church planting so that we plant one district church per year, one slum church and one "Antioch Team" church. It's a tall order, but we are now at the place where we have more leaders at the chapel than we know what to do with, and so we want to empower and export them! Putting a solid team around Steve has proved to be relatively easy. We want people to begin understanding that if they are involved—it is so that they can learn, and leave! That is easier said than done, but it is basic to our leadership development philosophy, and it has begun to bear fruit.

Fifth, *we plan to leave behind a solid legacy of Christian institutions for the next generation.* We want to begin schools, street-children's homes, orphanages, old people's homes, and Bible schools. We have therefore put together a team of people whose ministry will be to look for large tracts of land for purchase or to solicit as a donation to the church. Already we have a small core of people praying about starting a children's home. I am in discussion with an organization here about starting a school jointly with us. We are excited about what God is doing here and are looking to charge out into the future! God bless you all!

Perimeter Church. Our second case study is a church in Atlanta, Georgia. Perimeter Church was founded in 1978 by the Reverend Randy Pope. Randy's vision was to saturate Atlanta with vibrant churches that are true to the Scriptures and concerned for the non-kingdom people, both in their neighborhoods and around the world. Its larger vision is to glorify God by making mature believers for the lost world. Church leadership carefully framed their mission in support of this vision: to become a healthy, team-based church providing excellent resources for celebration, community, class and commission; and to partner with Perimeter Ministries and nationals to aggressively start churches in other communities and countries.

Because of their vision and mission, their Global Outreach Ministry was one of the foundations upon which the church was begun. Their first world missions program, however, was typical of many evangelical churches at that time. Missionaries approached the church, were evaluated on their call and their projected ministry, and supported financially and prayerfully as they went overseas under one of many sending agencies. A campus evangelistic ministry was the agency most frequently supported by Perimeter because of its emphasis on reaching nonkingdom people.

In 1985, through this agency, Perimeter was introduced to the ministry in Moscow in the Soviet Union. The church accepted the challenge to provide the financial backing for a New Life Training Center on the condition that Perimeter people could be involved in more ways than just sending dollars. As waves of Perimeter people spent time in Moscow during the last days of the Communist period, they built relationships with Russians and eventually connected with one who was burdened to go beyond evangelism and plant churches. This placed him outside the student ministry mandate, and when he resigned his position in that ministry, Perimeter became the facilitator of his vision. There was an immediate recognition of the greater effectiveness, passion and vision of a national than an expatriate missionary. This began a new direction for the Perimeter Global Outreach, facilitating the vision of nationals to reach their own people.

In the intervening years, building on this experience, *strategic partnerships* have been established with nationals in Poland, Albania, Guatemala, Mexico, Pakistan and Uzbekistan, and are being developed in Tanzania, India and China. All of these are church-planting/church-multiplication ministries.

A team of Perimeter lay people serves each of these strategic partnerships. Their responsibilities include praying for and serving the needs of the partner and the partnership. The leader of the team is considered to be a "non-resident missionary," and there is an equipping program to enable him or her to both develop the relationships and gain the competencies required to serve the partner effectively. The equipping includes regular weekly training in cross-cultural, missiological and ministry issues, using both training resources developed by Perimeter and other equipping agencies—both formal and informal. It is expected that the leader from Perimeter or his designee will be on the ground with the partner at least once and preferably twice a year.

What we especially notice are the values that drive these partnerships. The first is *servanthood*. Perimeter leaders watch for a national who has a burden to begin a church-planting movement, rather than plant an individual church. They see themselves as serving his or her vision and passion. The person on site is the leader, while they are the servants. Second, they seek to recognize the principle of *reciprocity*. As the leaders of Perimeter interact with the strategic partner and forge the partnership, they are alert for benefits that might accrue both for the overseas ministry and for Perimeter Church. Minimally they will want Perimeter people to be "on the ground" with the partner so as to forge international relationships that will impact their congregation in its understanding of the world, its prayer and financial commitments. Finally, they want their partnerships to be *strategic*. Perimeter partners are careful to research the country and environment as part of the partnership development, and watch for the strategic contribution to church expansion worldwide. In many countries, especially those in the so-called 10/40 window, this must be entry-level evangelism. In other countries they look for countrywide strategies and cooperation across a broad spectrum of theological and denominational distinctives. This has produced strategic partners that cover the spectrum from Baptist to charismatic, even though Perimeter itself is affiliated with the Presbyterian Church in America.

But according to Carl L. Wilhelm, the current director of Perimeter's Global Outreach, the most exciting development has occurred only recently. This has been the growing involvement of Perimeter in the developing missions of the Two-Thirds World. One of their ministry partners in Guatemala, ministering to the poor in the rural villages via medicine, is also a pastor in one of the largest churches in Guatemala City—which by June 1999 had grown to an attendance of over seventeen thousand. Through an unusual series of events, this pastor and his family were invited to join a Perimeter short-term journey to Pakistan on the condition that he secure at least seventy prayer supporters from his church. This visit took place in November and December 1997. God opened the eyes of these Guatemalan brothers and sisters in Karachi, and they returned to their church with a passion to launch their own world missions program. While active in the evangelization of Guatemala City, they had not yet developed a world perspective of missions.

In June 1998 Perimeter assisted in organizing and holding the first ever world missions conference at the La Iglesia Lluvias de Gracia, a church in Guatemala City, which turned out to be a first for the entire denomination. Two thousand people responded to the invitation to be involved—the vast majority expressing willingness to go to the Muslim world as missionaries. Subsequently, Perimeter partners enabled the church to form a missions committee, establish a screening and equipping program for those who responded by pointing them to resources and ministries capable of meeting their needs.

In 1999 Perimeter invited the Lluvias Church to send Guatemalans on the short-term missions journeys that they were organizing. During this year Guatemalans and Perimeter people will be together in Pakistan, Uzbekistan, India, China and Albania ministering with national partners in a broad spectrum of ministries, from direct evangelism to prayer journeys. In all, there will be more than 250 Perimeter-Lluvias adults overseas this year and an additional 100 youth.

Since the beginning of Perimeter, the Global Outreach staff has grown to seven people, handling more than $1.5 million. But more important than these impressive figures is their central calling to explore partnerships wherever their serving might enable a part of the church worldwide to accomplish a vision and enable a passion. Week by week, and through their annual missions's week emphasis, they seek to challenge the five thousand who attend the church to become world Christians. The challenge is great—too many of the Perimeter members are monocultural, unaware of either the need for the gospel in the world, or the magnificent work of God in expanding his church. But an important beginning has been made whereby a world church is growing through a mutual exchange of gifts.

6

....

The Missions Agency
Time for a Renaissance

Bud Anderson sank into his comfortable office chair after the first day of the annual board meeting of Global Harvest Mission (GHM). He agonizingly reviewed what took place earlier that day in the adjoining conference room. Report after report; debates over the theological qualifications of two missionary candidates; quibbling over details of expenditures. And on it went. Somehow he managed to endure, but his anxieties and discontent continued to grow. "What shall I do, Lord? We are so bogged down in detail that we are missing the big picture. What will happen if I share what really is on my heart?"

Bud's gloom the next morning was matched only by the heavy clouds and drenching rain that were all too obvious as he left his house. The first item on the agenda was the annual report from the general director. Normally this is an upbeat session full of optimism testifying to God's faithfulness. But this report was to be different, and Bud agonized over whether he was doing the right thing. Nevertheless, he put aside his prepared text and decided to become vulnerable and share his fears and convictions that the mission is close to going off track altogether.

Bud's first words jolted everyone into full alertness. "This may be the year in which God wants the Global Harvest Mission to close its doors." He went on to point out the uphill struggle for financial survival as well as the notable decline in both the quantity and quality of career missionary candidates. His sobering challenge was to ask everyone to consider prayerfully whether this is a message from God.

For the next hour he reviewed what was happening in the world and the radically changing role for U.S. missions boards. He shared how the old ways of working with churches are passing. In short, he focused with wisdom and insight on how the GHM and its counterparts find themselves caught in rapidly changing paradigms with little in the way of a roadmap to follow. He also shared fears about his own leadership skills and motivation.

As he sat down there were many moments of silence. The first response came from a veteran board member, the founding chair, who voiced his conviction that Bud was close to abandoning the heart vision of GHM. He argued strongly for restoration of faith that God is still seeking the lost and saw no reason whatsoever for Bud's pessimism, which he referred to as "needless breast-beating." There were several audible amens as he finished, especially from a handful of invited GHM senior missionaries. Although Bud empathized with what was said, his spirit sank as he realized the magnitude of the gap between himself and some key members of the board and the missionary community.

The next person to speak surprised everyone, however. Even though this was her first meeting, Mary Ann Evans, a GHM "missionary kid" who now was a corporate executive with an M.B.A. degree, strongly defended Bud. "I think what Bud did today took great courage. He is looking at the world through the eyes of God and has concluded that our old ways are no longer effective. He is calling for a review from top to bottom and sees the need for change. This is what a CEO is supposed to do, and I for one support him wholeheartedly."

That seemed to be exactly the catalyst needed. Another voice quickly added, "We are caught in yesterday's ruts. No wonder our income is dropping." There were other supportive voices. But then one person began to pray, and soon all were on their knees before God.

This remarkable prayer session went on for more than an hour, and there was consensus that Bud and the chair should appoint a vision task force composed of two board members and eight members of the missions community. This task force was given six months to undergo a thorough analysis of the mission, starting from its history and statement of purpose on through an assessment of the external world environment and missions resources. The challenge given was to provide a practical plan of action for the future.

*   *   *

HERE WE SEE A MAN OF GOD WHO COURAGEOUSLY FACED REAL storm clouds on the horizon. Together he and the board acted in the most responsible way by refusing to hold on to the past and daring to become risktakers. In so doing GHM has joined a growing number of churches and other agencies.

Bud has the mandate, of course, to make this task force a reality. He knew full well that one possible outcome would be to close the mission and cease operations altogether. Yet he is aware that there is a great deal of staff potential that, if tapped, could bring about significant change. Bud also is a realist. He knows that he might not be equipped to lead a "new GHM." While he is not anxious to step down, he is long past the stage of seeking and retaining a position just for the sake of power. In fact, he has told God that his only desire is to serve in the most appropriate way, regardless of position.

Facing a Clouded Future

There is no mistaking the fact that Western world missions is facing a clouded future. We have tried to make the case that today's dilemma is only a symptom of a much deeper problem—inability to cope with changing paradigms. In fact, much existing strategy and practice still harks back to the days when modernity was in full swing. Bill Ogden, general director of South America Mission (SAM) speaks right to the heart of the issue: "The task as viewed by the evangelical movement changed from *transforming the nations* [italics ours] to preparing 'some' from every tribe and nation to be rescued by the rapture."[1] This is a far cry from the mandate from Jesus Christ to extend his spiritual kingdom on earth.

In addition, existing structures and outlooks are to an alarming extent a product of the forces that shaped an earlier epoch. While denominational mission boards were dominant from the original Great Awakening through the middle of the nineteenth century, the primary legacy of today is the "faith mission movement," which is built on the foundation of volunteers who are willing to trust God for their very livelihood.

Nearly a century ago the Student Volunteer Movement mobilized large numbers who responded to the cry of its founder, John R. Mott, to "finish the work of the Great Commission in this generation." The same call has intensified at the dawn of a new millennium through the words of such missions statespersons as Ralph Winter, who boldly proclaims that "Never have the stakes been so high, or the opportunity so great. Never before has it been so impellingly possible for us to give our utmost for His highest."[2] Who is expected to provide the major share of funds and personnel? Why North America, of course.[3]

At the very foundation of the faith movement is *missionary-sending churches.* The pass-through model discussed in the previous chapter still is dominant, with the outcome that churches have come to see their world missions responsibility fulfilled once candidates are sent and financially supported. Little or no effort has been made, until recently, to hold either the missionary or the agency accountable. This, of course, all but abrogates God's conception of world missions as the reason for any church to exist.

Today we find literally hundreds of agencies facing major storm clouds as they look to the future. Here are the sobering conclusions from a recent study of one hundred mission boards[4]:

☐ There is undeniable acceleration in evangelism and church planting at the dawn of a new millennium, but the United States and other Western countries are far back in the pack insofar as leadership, initiative, momentum and contribution are concerned.

☐ North American Christian financial commitment to world missions is in sharp retrenchment.

☐ Most mission agencies anticipate expansion to meet world need but also face the discouraging prospect that financial resources will fall short of need if current trends are maintained.

The answers to this crisis are not likely to be found through impassioned appeals calling for sacrificial service and giving or speculative invective, which attempts to infuse the new millennium with an end-times eschatological significance. The solution can only come through a sweeping *renaissance*—a rebirth from the ashes of modernity that transforms missions theology, vision and strategy. In short, it is time to face the winds of the future in exactly the same fashion as Bud Anderson and his GHM team.

Organizational Transformation

As we pointed out in chapter four, if missions is to adapt, it must be: (1) sensitive to the initiative of God, (2) motivated by a vision of the reign of Christ as refracted through the multiple cultures of the world, (3) characterized by mutual sharing from multiple centers of influence and (4) committed to partnership and collaboration. For this to happen among agencies, nothing short of a top-down, bottom-up organizational *transformation* is necessary.

The American business world has led the way at the end of the twentieth century through a wrenching and often traumatic transformation process motivated by such well-known authors as Drucker,[5] Peters[6] and Senge.[7] The outcome has been a startling resurgence in productivity and innovation, which has led to unprecedented levels of economic growth and competitiveness. Why has this taken place? It is simply because the pressures of declining profit—the bottom line—have left no option.

American industry slumped in its productivity because of outmoded hierarchical structures that inhibited vitally needed innovation through a command and control style of leadership that stifled managerial initiative. Often within a period of months, sweeping organizational transformation took place that began with a top-down commitment to empower and unleash innovation and productivity. Products and services were eliminated on a massive scale as they were shown to be competitively inferior. This, of course, was accompanied by extensive downsizing, but the outcomes over a very short period of years have been unprecedented.

There are some who will object that comparing secular industry with Christian churches and enterprises is entirely inappropriate. Perhaps, but there are startling similarities. Both are victims of the same root problems: (1) a lack of focus on the bottom line and (2) a lagging commitment to making people productive and fulfilled. Yes, there are differences between profit-motivated organizations and Christian agencies, but both require an organizational transformation that encompasses five essential steps:

1. *Restoration*—an infusion and wholehearted acceptance of clarified core values throughout the institution. In the context of world missions, this requires a renouncement of the influence of modernity in missions strategy and theology and the restoration of the reign of Christ as the motivation for faith and action.

2. *Convergence*—a clarification and refocusing of organizational core values and purpose in the context of current world realities and eternal truth.

3. *Regeneration*—an unleashing of organizational resources through empowerment and leadership development.

4. *Adaptation*—a creative and revitalized response of adapting strategy to meet a changing environment. Ideally this takes place in a Christian enterprise only when it is motivated and energized by the Holy Spirit.

5. *Reengineering*—enhanced effectiveness and efficiency through modified structures and procedures.

Transformation requires a no-holds-barred recognition by the board and top leadership that status quo is simply not an option. This requires courage and faith, because the process that is launched will never become a reality in an agency characterized by timidity, unexamined traditionalism, internal dissension and division, or resistance to change. So we must say to our colleagues from missions agencies, *the ball is in your court*. There is no automatic formula to follow, but one thing is certain—God rewards those who diligently seek the best for his kingdom.

Restoration. Managerial missiology places great premium on strategic thinking and planning which has two related objectives which build on one another—(1) *doing the right things* and (2) *doing things right*. Unfortunately we are all too prone to put the cart before the horse and wind up doing the wrong things more effectively.

The worst possible action is to retain outmoded paradigms of world missions and perpetuate the corrupting influence of modernity on biblical truth. We, of course, strongly believe that the reign of Christ is the theological rock on which world missions is built, and this needs no further elaboration here. While you may not agree with our exposition and application, we urge the entire world missions enterprise to engage once again in genuine theological reflection, accompanied by prayer and fasting. If this step is not taken, the remainder of the transformation process has little value. Uncertainty at this point may result in a house built on sand.

The objective is to establish and clarify a set of core values that truly reflect a missiology that is both biblical and relevant for the contemporary world. Core values are the *nonnegotiable cornerstones on which the ministry enterprise is built*. Often these core values are assumed and not articulated with clarity. What that means, of course, is that there is no clear theological rudder to keep the enterprise on course.

Core values, at the very minimum, must embrace these essential considerations:

☐ clear exegesis of the Great Commission with particular focus on biblical holism and discipleship

☐ sensitivity to cultural changes and a responsiveness to providential opportunities

☐ understanding of the role for the local church in the total framework of organizational vision

☐ dedication to practices whereby all members of the organization family are made productive and fulfilled

☐ commitment to partnerships and alliances whereby worldwide ministry will function as mutually related centers of influence

The kind of analytical reflection required here needs input from all ranks of the organization. Board members and senior leaders must listen carefully and seek discernment from the Holy Spirit. The process also requires an extended time period. It culminates in a statement of theological convictions and core values that, after considerable input, is put in place and utilized as the absolute bedrock of all functions and actions.

If this sounds a bit grandiose and impractical, consider the fact that World Vision International, Society for International Ministries (SIM), Mission Aviation Fellowship, Operation Mobilization and many others have done precisely this. Furthermore, the process never can be considered finished. Core values must be reexamined at frequent intervals. One organization that was established in 1995, Development Associates International, undertook this process once again in 1999 and was greatly benefitted by some significant clarification, accompanied by strengthened unity in its staff family.

Convergence. Once a proper theological platform is in place, the next step is to move forward to bring a greater convergence between organizational vision/mission and current world realities. Here are three related questions that, if taken seriously, will drive to the very bedrock:

1. What difference would it make on the world scene if the agency were to cease existence?

2. What difference would it make to churches in the sending country if the agency were to cease existence?

3. What can we contribute to the body of Christ as it is presently ministering among a people group so that it will extend the kingdom in a discernible way?

The intent, of course, is to verify the extent to which an existing vision or missions statement is valid given the contemporary world environment. Many long-established mission boards still embrace a vision dating back many decades that calls for pioneer church planting. Missionaries are still sent to various fields as they always have been. While we do not deny the need for church planting, the scene today is radically different, given the growth of mission-sending churches and agencies from the original receiving countries. The initiative here rightly belongs with those who have the greatest cultural affinity and understanding. We are disturbed by the continuing flood of church planting teams into various people groups in the world. This happened with unfortunate results in Russia, where missions have operated without coordination and in almost total disregard of context—both cultural and ecclesiastical.

Our point is this: a central consideration in the vision of any North American or Western agency today must be: How do we relate to the body of Christ in a particular area of the world so that, leaving behind any intent to control, we can contribute constructively within an alliance of cooperating organizations? As we have repeatedly stressed, North America is just one, albeit often a significant, participant along with others who by call, gifting or cultural affinity have an equal or even greater role to play. It is time to follow our Lord, who modeled a servanthood that places the considerations of others above our own.

We suggest the following component be incorporated into either the core values or the vision statement of agencies whose roots go back several decades or more: *we covenant not to launch ministry in any part of the world without first dialoging with churches and others ministering there to discover what we might contribute to the totality of ministry if we work together in alliance.* One well-known agency followed precisely this practice in a country where the mission was forced to withdraw by the country's national church. A leadership team from the mission sat down once again with the current national leaders and asked this question with a real spirit of servanthood. They were welcomed to return, this time in a spirit of partnership as equals, providing resource people who can spearhead leadership development and participate in discipleship training among local churches.

The Africa Inland Mission (AIM) also followed this practice when it first entered Mozambique in the middle of the 1980s. The usual policy of planting its own churches was put aside in favor of working under a broader umbrella to provide a service to a number of churches. This evolved into a plan by which AIM negotiates with individual denominations for specific ways of undertaking joint ministries. This policy has contributed significantly to the rapid development of the church with the result that AIM is now one of the largest agencies in the country.

The importance of outcome evaluations. It is not unusual to discover that a mission agency has too little relevant information available to answer the diagnostic questions with any certainty. This, of course, is a clear signal that outcomes are not taken seriously—a real danger sign. On other occasions it is not uncommon to find a uniformly positive answer to diagnostic questions, which in fact reflects an uncritical acceptance of organizational propaganda more than anything else. This too is totally unacceptable. In both situations the only remedy is to turn immediately to the neglected evaluative homework.

Let's continue with the story of GHM. The vision task force wisely devoted much energy to focused information gathering from staff, supporting churches and recipients of ministry. Then they were in a position to answer the three questions above. The task force conclusion was that they would not perpetuate the life of this agency today for the reason that it had become irrelevant in much of its ministry. They went on to conclude that the agency's impact had declined to the point that there would be little discernible difference if the doors were closed.

The present GHM statement of vision calls for "completion of the Great Commission through bringing the good news to the lost and planting churches." But there was overwhelming evidence that the primary outcome in recent years has been maintenance of existing institutionalized churches that do little more than perpetuate superficial Christianity. There was a consensus that church revitalization and spiritual formation must jump to the forefront of GHM priorities.

The relationships with supporting churches also suggested a genuine need for change. In fact, pastors and lay leaders voiced many of the same concerns about GHM as those expressed by Sally Calderone and her committee at First Church. It became painfully clear that today's growing financial crisis at GHM will only intensify as churches become more proactive in fulfilling their world missions imperative.

Facing the imperative to change. What the task force discovered, of course, is a missions agency whose vision and strategies, while entirely appropriate at earlier periods, have not changed to keep pace with today's realities. So what are the options? This question can only be answered if all of the stakeholders—the board, the executive staff, the missionaries and donors—are willing to address the need for change head-on.

Boards
A critical element that affects openness to change is the board. Boards exist for one central reason—to insure that the agency is fulfilling its vision with excellence and integrity. Unfortunately, the board sometimes is more of an impediment than an initiator. A conservative mentality can prevail, which leads to maintenance of tradition, status quo and preservation of financial resources. Effective boards cannot avoid moving from safe ground in the face of compelling needs if its Christian responsibilities are taken seriously.

The Chief Executive Officer
John Kotter has discovered that successful generation of change is largely the product of a leadership style that is motivational and influential.[8] It has far less to do with such managerial functions as planning, budgeting, organizing and problem solving. The CEO must provide a searchlight of vision, challenge and empowerment that moves beyond words to visible and consistent action. In other words, memos and chapel messages will have little or no value without hands-on relationships and involvement by the CEO.

Fortunately, Bud Anderson has not followed the style of his predecessor, who rarely was accessible in day-to-day operations. Bud met weekly with the members of the vision task force and did his best to be vulnerable where necessary as well as supportive. His door was open to any with opposing viewpoints, and he experienced some difficult moments. Nonetheless the staff at the end of the process applauded him for his love, forthrightness and unwavering vision.

As Bud soon discovered, however, the process of implanting vision and motivating change is rarely orderly or predictable. In fact, it is messy, ambiguous, fraught with setbacks and rarely achieved within a timetable. If change is to take place, the CEO must tolerate ambiguity, uncertainty and even fear.

Fortunately our experience with agency CEOs, most of whom are not founders or dominant leaders from the past, provides genuine optimism that nearly all are willing to serve as a champion of change. In fact, Kotter states that the biggest obstacle is likely to be those just a notch or two below the CEO.[9] These often are the ones with the most to lose.

Missionaries and Staff

In organizational transformation it is entirely possible that positions will be eliminated, projects canceled or fields abandoned. This never is pleasant, and tensions of this nature are almost unavoidable, especially among veteran missionaries and staff who have not been equipped to cope with changing realities. Unless careful precautions are taken, the process of transformation quickly can become sabotaged and even derailed by pressure groups and power blocks. The most important consideration is to insure that all whose lives and ministries will be affected are (1) listened to with integrity and concern and (2) given a guarantee that genuine safety nets are available if needed.

Donors

All financial contributors are free to vote with their pocketbooks, just as First Church did when we first joined them. Bud was dismayed to discover that three large donors had been alerted by two prominent field leaders that the vision task force was about to capitulate to theological liberalism. Bud visited all three and received a warning in no uncertain terms that future giving would be jeopardized if their voices were not heard. Each was fully aware that GHM would lose more than 20 percent of its financial support if their threats were carried out.

Bud took their comments seriously and even was tempted to put the vision process on an indefinite hold. Nonetheless, he did not yield. Instead he patiently discussed all that was happening and tried to explain the rationale behind some of the changes he envisioned. Two of the three listened with interest, even to the point of expressing genuine appreciation for his patience and concern, and providing assurance that they would continue and even increase their financial giving. The other individual responded with hostility and made his threat an actuality. Bud fortunately had anticipated that this probably would take place and was unwilling to sacrifice integrity for strictly financial reasons.

The important lesson to be learned here is the need for ongoing communication with all agency donors and stakeholders. Soon GHM's communication department prepared a series of documents and updates, which were sent to everyone on the mailing list along with a request for feedback. Telephone conferences and personal meetings were held with many who expressed concern, and the task force members were delighted with the wisdom provided in these dialogues.

Making Convergence Become a Reality

There are three possible outcomes of the process: (1) closing the doors, (2) maintaining status quo, and (3) renewing and clarifying the vision.

Closing the doors. There are times where option one, shutting down, is the best decision. After all, God has never promised eternal life to any Christian agency other than the church itself. Mission Aviation Fellowship faced this as a distinct possibility given the fact that the need for missionary aviation in pioneer fields was apparently beginning to ebb. In that case one option was to close, celebrate what God has done and distribute remaining resources to others. This was seriously considered, even to the point that top leadership contemplated a celebration of rejoicing that the need at MAF's founding had been met.

It is our conviction that the option of closing down, or at least seriously retrenching, should be viewed by all agencies, regardless of their lengths of existence, as a very real option. In fact, it is an imperative for both the board and top management to verify on an ongoing basis that the agency has earned the right to continue to exist. *The only way this assessment can be made is on the basis of the continued fulfillment of its mission and vision as measured by concrete outcomes.*

It is interesting that many of today's newly formed "niche agencies" (i.e., those formed to meet a specialized need in today's environment) are committed to continued ministry only as long as the need has not been met. Many of these are dedicated to training and consulting with the goal of transferring skills and abilities to the point where they are most needed. Once this goal is achieved within target areas, the organizational wineskin will be discarded and resources freed for other purposes.

One reviewer of this book spoke for other thoughtful critics who suggested that all North American and European agencies should embark on an immediate process to close all ministries within a four-year period. From one perspective, this is completely understandable given the emergence and vitality of missions movements throughout the Two-Thirds World. Furthermore, it is easy to conclude that necessary transformation cannot and will not take place soon enough in historic sending countries.

Nonetheless, we wholeheartedly affirm the necessity of mutual sharing from multiple centers of influence whereby the church worldwide works through alliances to share resources Christ has provided in his kingdom. This will not happen, of course, if long established agencies continue historic patterns of dominance and control; but neither will it happen if they go out of existence! In any case, we are encouraged that needed change is well underway.

Maintaining status quo. In today's world one thing is certain—agencies and missions-minded churches do not have the right of continued existence in world ministry if they are perpetuating the disabling liabilities from modernity that we have identified in these pages.

The vision task force at GHM could have hunkered down in a

status quo mentality, but this never was seen as a valid option. There was a consensus that it was far better either to close down in a way that honors God or focus on a change of vision that will bring about convergence with the needs of all stakeholders.

Renewing and clarifying the vision. The vision task force at GHM elected to launch an organizational renaissance and proposed a new statement of vision that was worded in this way:

> In response to the mandate of Jesus Christ to extend his kingdom on earth, GHM is dedicated to joining hands with national churches and missions agencies to plant, build and nurture churches that, by their life and actions, seek to follow faithfully Jesus Christ and to draw others to him.

This proposed vision statement then was evaluated and modified slightly through extensive discussion with missionaries, staff and donors. With few exceptions, all who were consulted felt affirmed that their voice was heard and carefully considered. Later this became the official vision statement for the movement worldwide. In effect, it provided an all-new rudder for the movement in the changed seas of today.

Similarly, Mission Aviation Fellowship reevaluated the richness of resources it could offer to the world and discovered previously unrecognized opportunities to capitalize on technological skill and capability that moves beyond air transportation. The outcome was establishment of a division that has exponentially increased worldwide access and use of information technology and the Internet.

GHM, of course, is a hypothetical mission, and the discussion here, by necessity, is brief. The process normally will require many months of patient listening and response. Nonetheless the approach can have an amazing outcome as directions are focused and new energy infused into the ministry.

Regeneration

Regeneration is a vital stage because it is here that human resources are empowered, enabled and released for purposes of creative innovation following the Holy Spirit. There are two diagnostic questions that should help you evaluate current realities:

1. Are major strategic decisions made in the field subject to review and ratification at a centralized source before implementation steps are taken?

2. Is a staff development plan in place for each missionary and leader to facilitate ongoing personal growth and skill enhancement and to identify future leaders?

The first of these questions addresses the freedom given for field initiative. International businesses are increasingly discovering that maximum autonomy must be provided for scattered entities to chart their own course. A small, centralized executive staff grants such autonomy, though it is first subject to the mandate that all actions must be consistent with and enhance a clearly defined statement of vision and mission. The second qualification is that all field units are held totally accountable for projected outcomes. Therefore, no free rein is given for field units to adopt what Jim Plueddemann refers to as a "wildflower" mentality based on a "go-with-the-flow" approach that is devoid of serious planning and accountability.[10]

Do not fail to miss the implications of what is said here. Freedom to chart a relevant course is a virtual necessity for enterprises characterized by widely scattered operating entities. *For this to take place, a definitive, well-thought-through mission statement must be in place and used, without exception, as the roadmap guiding all strategic initiatives.* Furthermore, authority and responsibility should be delegated to responsible leaders who are subject to rigorous standards of accountability. This requires clearly defined objectives and outcomes. Finally, top management must be fully committed to an ongoing strategy of leadership development designed to empower those in the field to chart their own course with integrity and excellence.

Few missions organizations meet the above standards. Here are just a few of many unfortunate outcomes that litter the history of missions:

1. Field autonomy characterized by irresponsible "free rein," where staff go their own way with little accountability and commitment to organizational mission. It is not uncommon for such a spirit to be rationalized by the specious declaration that "I work

only for the Lord and not for you."

2. Field autonomy granted to field leaders who have had little or no further training and leadership development beyond seminary or graduate school. In this case, top leaders have all but abrogated their responsibility to insure that others are equipped to assume the responsibilities they are given.

3. A tight rein whereby all major field initiatives can be ratified only after clearing a series of approval hurdles. Sometimes this begins with a field council that has veto power. Then the next hurdle may be a distant, over-extended regional leader. And on it goes to headquarters. By the time all hurdles are cleared, the original initiative may be barely recognizable, and the opportunity is lost. It also is almost guaranteed that those in the field either will capitulate in a spirit of defeat or undertake "end-runs" based on the fact that it is easier to ask for forgiveness than approval.

The corporate world once again is leading the way to enlightened empowerment through adoption of team management, whereby functional specialists join on a temporary or ongoing basis and are given authority and responsibility to develop and market new products and services. The goal, of course, is to achieve a professional synergism around a shared vision and goal that is almost impossible otherwise. Teams of this nature are especially valuable at the field level.

Bud Anderson recognized at the outset that the transformation required an all-out team effort. The vision task force was carefully chosen to achieve a balance of temperaments, experience and expertise. The task force itself elected a leader who functioned primarily as a coordinator, in recognition that creativity can only thrive in a free-rein environment without hierarchical processes.

Finally, Bud did not miss the unmistakable necessity for an organization-wide program of leadership development. At one point in GHM's history nearly all missionaries became pastors in the field, thus making Bible school or seminary education a necessity. Fortunately the leadership team had already recognized that the need for missionary pastoral skills has dwindled as national churches have matured. GHM had the courage to recognize that it is time to move beyond this vestigial remain from an earlier era and recognize that a world characterized by blinding rapidity of technological and cultural change requires ongoing professional development. It has become painfully obvious, for example, that outcomes assessment is nearly impossible unless field missionaries are adequately trained and equipped.

Few boards have taken leadership development seriously, other than to encourage mid-career missionaries to devote their leaves to graduate or seminary study. While this can be of some value, true leadership development takes place primarily on the job, where relevant learning is acquired and applied under the guidance of mentors. Moreover, it is ongoing rather than sporadic.

Development Associates International is one professional network that has emerged to meet this need through field-based, learner-directed, nonformal education on both a credit and noncredit basis worldwide. But their experience to date has demonstrated beyond doubt that Two-Thirds World organizations recognize the need and respond far more readily than their Western counterparts. The most common source of resistance is unwillingness to make leadership development a part of the job description of each missionary and staff person because of the greater priority and sense of urgency to "fulfill the task" in the shortest possible time.

Leadership development, after all, is nothing more than an extension of Christ's mandate to make disciples. We ask with some dismay why this priority, so central in the life of our Lord, seems to be obscured in our obsession to turn the Great Commission into a great commotion.

It seems pretty obvious that the underlying issue is a theological worldview infected with elements of a modern worldview. Change can begin only when this problem is brought to the surface and recognized honestly. It is reported that Martin Luther once was asked what he would do if the Lord were to return tomorrow. His response? *"I would plant a tree!"* We would be well advised to assume a similar long-term perspective and do likewise with our leaders.

Adaptation

When commitment to change is demonstrated and an empowering outlook is in place, the next stage is to adapt the ministry strategy to the changing environment following the leadership of the Holy Spirit. Four diagnostic questions are helpful at this stage:

1. Are major strategic initiatives based on a realistic understanding of the opportunities and challenges faced in each field?

2. What would happen to the field ministry if each program or function within the ministry were phased out?

3. What changes could be made in ministry programs to make them more effective?

4. Is strategic planning undertaken on the assumption that sufficient funds can be raised from donors to facilitate continued ministry growth?

The Evangelical Free Church was compelled to address these issues in the early 1990s when it was forced to evacuate Zaire, historically its largest field of ministry. To the surprise of some, the indigenous church continued to thrive under adverse conditions. Even though most missionaries were allowed to reenter the country, the Evangelical Free Church Mission (EFCM) wisely decided to withdraw most of its Zaire-based personnel. This led to a rethinking of the entirety of the mission's role across Africa.

A former seminary professor in the Central African Republic was appointed to spearhead research on new ministry opportunities among existing churches and missions throughout Africa. Two of the many new initiatives that surfaced: working with Sudanese refugees in Northern Uganda and a cooperative church plant among the Asian community in Dar-es-Salaam, Tanzania.

As the EFCM quickly discovered, each of the above questions is fraught with tension-causing and potentially explosive implications, but the issues raised cannot be avoided by any agency taking biblical stewardship seriously. And wrestling with them honestly can issue in creative initiatives that otherwise would have been overlooked.

A Realistic Understanding of Field Challenges

Very few readers would disagree that strategic thinking must be based on valid information, accompanied by creative adaptation of strategy. Nonetheless, we still face a veritable flood of standardized, Western-initiated programs—especially prepackaged evangelistic strategies. This problem is compounded by a continuation of centrally directed field ministries that discourage localized adaptation. The outcome all-too-frequently is a strategic misfire. Fortunately there are enough exceptions to this generalization to provide genuine hope for the future, but the need for change still looms large.

It is helpful once again to stress that strategic decisions are based on three foundational considerations: (1) experience that has been analyzed and interpreted, (2) a reliable intuition, and (3) information on current realities. Picture these as a three-legged stool solidly grounded in the leadership provided by the Holy Spirit. If any of the legs is removed, the stool will fall.

It is virtually impossible, in the first place, to face field challenges without at least some reliance on experience. But notice that we have added two important qualifiers if experience is to have strategic value—*analyzed* and *interpreted*. There is the old story of a field missionary with twenty years of experience that, in reality, represented one year repeated twenty times. If experience is to have validity, there must be continual assessment of outcomes, accompanied by a heart attitude of learning how to be more effective. Only then are essential lessons learned that can be used meaningfully in the future.

God also provides each of us with a sense of intuition that must be seriously considered if it is guided by sensitivity to the Holy Spirit. We often notice, for example, that there are some who seem to have a consistent sense of what should be done, which is then verified by outcomes. At times this can come in the form of a supernaturally guided prophetic message. It is far more likely, however, to emerge as a quiet conviction. We cannot fail to put these admittedly subjective inputs on the table in a team context because this may be the manner in which the still, small voice of God surfaces.

Finally, we cannot avoid the example of Jesus, who did his field homework by living among those in need, listening with sensitivity, and responding under the guidance of the Holy Spirit. Contemporary missiology has recognized the need for valid research, and there are many sources that provide helpful guidance in ethnological and survey research.

When these three legs of the stool are in place, the decision-makers, hopefully a gifted team, are in a strong position to venture forth with an entrepreneurial spirit. What this requires, of course, is an undergirding commitment to let go of unproductive programs and to adapt the remainder to speak more clearly to localized considerations.

No single leg in the stool can be considered as dominant, however. For example, nothing can be worse than a dogmatic insistence, often by an influential leader, that "God told me," or a rigid obstacle put in place by a veteran who loudly objects because of his experience a decade ago, or a freshly trained missiologist who demands that we must do what her research says. Each of these must be viewed as just one piece of a much-larger whole picture which only emerges as the Holy Spirit speaks to a team through prayer.

Once a decision team has a sense of direction, the process of implementation becomes all-important. Jim Plueddemann offers the wise counsel to approach implementation as a somewhat uncertain pilgrimage.[11] Uncertainty is inevitable because every strategic initiative requires a journey along a path often poorly marked and even potentially perilous. Progress on this journey requires a sense of vigilance and a willingness to respond to unexpected twists and turns. What this means is that any strategic plan must be held loosely, undergirded by a continuous attitude of reliance on the Holy Spirit, and modified where needed.

Surely it is now apparent why we raise such cautionary flags against the plethora of prepackaged programs of world evangelization that are "sold" internationally. Admittedly, some are of sufficient relevance and value to warrant immediate adoption in certain situations. Furthermore, most offer valuable elements that might be included within a larger strategic vision. Nonetheless, history amply testifies that an impulsive acceptance of prepackaged programs by those without strategic planning savvy can have disastrous, counterproductive effects that short-circuit the leadership of the Holy Spirit. God expects much more from his children, for he has endowed them with the resources and insights to extend his creativity.

The Urgency of Valid Outcomes Assessment

Joseph D'Souza, executive director of Operation Mobilization India, relates a compelling example of what he refers to as the "scandal of mission statistics."[12] A report was widely circulated by a particular indigenous organization that it had planted over ten thousand churches in North India. This allegedly occurred in tribal areas that have experienced decades of Christian growth. After twenty years, however, few of those churches were found to be in existence for the reason that a "church" was considered to be planted if members of a Bible study had gathered a number of times. In reality, there was no baptism, no eldership, no local church in any sense.

Here is another Indian example. One agency disseminated the glowing report that over 250,000 Christian books had been distributed among a largely unreached people group. Is distribution of books, in and of itself, an outcome? Hardly. No evidence was provided to document that these books were opened, read and responded to in discernible ways. That would have required some diligent visits and lengthy discussions among those who supposedly had "accepted" them.

We also provided yet another example in an earlier chapter where Global Harvest Mission reported a number of alleged converts from mass evangelism. What they had not assessed, however, is the number who persevered in church membership and were truly launched on a pilgrimage of spiritual growth, demonstrated by changes in outlook and behavior.

Each of these examples has a common element—completion of a programmatic event described in numerical terms. This is nothing more than a first step toward genuine outcomes assessment. Today we must ask *what happened because an event took place or an action was undertaken?*

We are especially suspicious of today's ongoing "evangelistic countdown," whereby the number of people in a given area who call themselves Christian is tracked over time. What does it mean to state that 40 percent now claim to be Christian? If we must have a "countdown," let's look at the changes through the eyes of Jesus. There should, for example, be demonstrable declines in dishonesty, immorality and oppression of the poor by the rich, accompanied by economic lift among the disadvantaged. The fact that evidence of this type is not collected and disseminated speaks for itself. Admittedly, outcomes of this nature are subjective and difficult to measure and quantify. Nevertheless such changes are visible in the life of a church that offers true hope to the downtrodden. All that is required is a willingness to look and to discern.

Programmatic Response

A proper programmatic response begins with a vision of the changes that would come about if a program were effective. A wise evangelist, for example, would move far beyond the numbers and envision the changes that ideally would take place in individual lives, in a church and in broader society. He or she would value an evangelistic response only as a first step toward genuine discipleship and spiritual maturity. This step, in itself, would broaden ministry horizons to embrace partnerships and alliances with local churches and agencies to insure that spiritual formation is taken seriously.

But now we reach one of those explosive issues where the rubber meets the road. Peter Drucker has long advocated a policy of *planned abandonment,* for the very reason that the world changes over time and renders once vital and well-conceived strategies obsolete. This is a fact that no amount of tinkering or investment can change. Common sense would suggest that programs be dropped when their time has come, but that rarely is done. It almost seems that missions strategies and programs are blessed with the assurance of eternal life.

Whether we are willing to accept it or not, program abandonment is an unavoidable necessity for those who take kingdom stewardship seriously. It is true, of course, that outcries of righteous indignation will surface, especially when jobs are changed or dropped altogether. Resistance to radical change is simply a part of human nature, but it can be minimized by finding relevant ways to put a real Christian safety net under those whose lives are affected. This is a far better option than to capitulate, leave well enough alone and perpetuate the "ailing baby" through maintenance of status quo. All this does is to postpone an effectiveness crisis that will surely escalate over time.

So what is the alternative? *Continually ask what difference it would make to ministry recipients if a given strategy or program is dropped.* Start by taking this question to the Lord and allow him to be the Lord of the Harvest, who prunes unproductive growth. In other words, function as pilgrims who always must check to make sure that they are on the right road and who are always willing to change course when necessary.

Becoming Galilean in Our Outlook and Approach

For many decades Mission, Inc., has tended to move from the Western center to the periphery, ablaze with technological firepower, large-scale programs and a visibly Western worldview. This clearly has been a case of the "haves" giving to the "have-nots," no matter how much we have been motivated by Christian love and compassion. Becoming *Galilean* means adopting a very different outlook and approach.

Galileans are pilgrims with a message that must be visibly incarnate to other seekers of the truth, and being Galilean is not defined by geography, wealth, education or technological sophistication. Pilgrims do not possess a "religious product" that must be marketed by skillfully persuasive firepower to an unreached world. Strategy, technology, numerical growth and resources are not driving considerations, because the pilgrim model is characterized by an unfailing commitment to *place people before programs.*

Process and relationships are more important than deadlines. There may be frustrating delays and side trips on the way. Prayer is more important than action. Servanthood and self-denial take the place of dominance and control. It is false to draw a dichotomy between evangelism and social transformation.

This pilgrimage also is fraught with human frailty, divisions and power motivation. Its participants are fallen individuals who struggle and fail. Its greatest strength, however, is faith and perseverance grounded in total reliance on the sovereignty of God. In the best sense of the word, it struggles to restore the very elements that are sometimes lost in Western modernity.

The goal is to develop disciples who function in Christian community as salt and light in the world. These points of light multiply, combine and spread as the people of God, with flaws and blemishes, join others in partnerships and alliances on a journey of faith with their Lord. Will Mission, Inc., find a place in this Galilean pilgrimage? Frankly, it is unlikely as long as the Western managerial juggernaut is perpetuated.

Pilgrims model a process that can only be dimly grasped and understood from within a Western worldview. All partners are equals through a spirit of mutual submission in a greater cause. Anyone will be accepted with open arms when they come as a servant, anxious to help enhance the effectiveness of others.

In short, the West is welcome on the pilgrimage only if there is a willingness to join as fellow Galileans in humility with strugglers who learn as they go and are willing to sacrifice a Western urgency to achieve kingdom-oriented outputs. A very different kind of missionary is required today—one who is willing to come in submission as an *enabler*, who serves by empowering others through an offering of much-needed gifts and skills that others do not possess.

The pilgrimage model will slowly but surely drive out churches or agencies who come in a spirit of triumphalism, imperialism or independence, whether their roots be in the West or in the Two-Thirds World. Those who hear the voice of the Master will quickly distinguish between the spirit of the world and the Spirit of God.

The Issue of Donor-Driven Strategies

Now we have entered the most dangerous minefield of all—fundraising. Do you remember our fundamental query, which asks, "Is strategic planning undertaken on the assumption that sufficient funds can be raised from donors to facilitate continued ministry growth?" On the surface, this appears quite harmless because it accurately describes an almost universal practice. Nonetheless, it is fraught with consequences.

First of all, continued growth cannot be taken as a given in the reign of Christ; there is no guarantee of divinely sanctioned permanence, *let alone financial support!* What this means is that any agency must justify its very existence and financial support, to say nothing of growth, on the basis of both need and performance. In many cases, the reverse order prevails.

Consider the case of Global Harvest Mission once again. Its current outlook and ministry evokes the optimism and pragmatism that characterized the post-World War II era. It is encumbered with an aging staff that sadly lacks the equipping so necessary to carry out the pilgrim model needed in today's alliances and partnerships. Furthermore, many of its missionaries still serve as pastors and in other forms of leadership that should have been taken over years ago by qualified nationals. Finally, the budget is encumbered with maintaining institutions the national church can ill afford to assume.

In short, *GHM has failed to adapt to changing times and now faces a financial crisis and a potent threat to its continued existence.* Fortunately, Bud and his board have seen the handwriting on the wall and have launched a much-needed process of organizational transformation. They could have chosen, instead, to undertake an intensified marketing-oriented fundraising effort similar to that which was so productive nearly twenty years ago.[13] What would this look like if that option had been chosen?

Certainly there would be a call upon supporting churches to increase their financial contributions. Individual donors would be contacted by telephone and personal visits, especially those who have given most generously in the past (curiously designated as "major donors"). Foundation proposals would be widely circulated.

But would so called "donor marketing" turn the tide in this situation? Probably not. A nearly across-the-board decline in financial support from churches and individuals reflects changing priorities and a growing suspicion that traditional missions no longer play a vital role.[14] While GHM might get a temporary boost from its donors past the age of sixty, most of the younger Christian world will not be receptive.

Bud, to his credit, sensed the futility of intensified fundraising as a solution to the GHM crisis. He wisely sensed that the financial slump could be a clear signal from God that change is needed. In response, he and the board have placed the entire ministry on God's altar as a living sacrifice. This took courage and forthrightness. We strongly urge others in similar crises to do the same in the assurance that the Lord is still Lord.

Having said that, however, let us again make clear that fundraising, properly conceived, is a valid ministry. The apostle Paul demonstrated in 2 Corinthians that financial generosity is a quality of all mature Christians (2 Cor 8—9). And true generosity is blessed by God. So all mature Christians should give in response to a prompting from their Lord. Christian agencies can perform a legitimate and needed ministry of informing prospective donors and making their needs known in an ethical and truthful manner.

It is unfortunate that overly zealous donor marketing has served to alienate a large portion of the Christian donor public by attempting to sell the *sizzle* rather than the *steak*.[15] It is especially tempting to fudge numbers to underscore the competitive superiority of what an agency has done. Fortunately, these practices seem, at long last, to have fallen into ill repute. Nevertheless, widespread disillusionment still prevails among potential donors, thus making legitimate fundraising even more difficult.

One often hears the lament in missions circles that the younger generation of Christians do not exhibit familiar patterns of giving. They are not interested in agencies that need long-term, continued support; they are much more likely to be attracted to shorter-term projects that are focused and effective. Most importantly, they are most likely to have an interest in programs in which they can be personally involved in some way. These postmoderns are clearly disillusioned with large, lethargic entities, and they can see through hype in a second. (Remember, they were reared on a steady diet of television.) By contrast, they are attracted to programs that feature hands-on partnerships and crosscultural relationships.

Rather than lamenting these changes, we advocate embracing them. In fact we are arguing that this style of giving best suits the newer forms of missions we are highlighting. Offer these people an opportunity to be involved in various ways. Lay out clearly the focus and timelines for the programs, and they will respond. Be assured that a successful conclusion of one project will lay the groundwork for support for the next.

What then should a responsible agency do in the face of financial need? We recommend the following steps:

1. *Begin by carefully considering what could be done in present or proposed ministries if there were no further funding.* God often expects us to work within existing resources and withholds funds for this reason alone. If a ministry is worth undertaking, ways will given by the Lord to proceed, regardless of donor response.

2. *If step one yields a persistent sense across a team of decision-makers that God has greater things in mind, the next step is to present these to him through individual and corporate prayer and fasting.* He is, after all, still Lord of the Harvest and fully capable of providing these resources with no effort on our parts. Many, including the authors, have seen graphic demonstrations of the power of God in this way. Why deny him the privilege of blessing us?

3. *Do not make needs known until there is a common agreement that God seems to have given the green light to do so.* Once the go ahead is given, proceed in confidence that you are giving others the great opportunity to extend their lives and ministries through you by financial participation. Donor research consistently reveals the blessings that come to donors in this way.[16]

4. *Never lose sight of the fact that only the Holy Spirit can motivate a response that is consistent with his will.* He is the persuader, not the communicator. All that the communicator can do is to give witness to what God himself wants to do. Anything else quickly borders on manipulation.

Reengineering

The last step in the transformation process, reengineering, is undertaken to enhance effectiveness and efficiency through modified structures and procedures.[17] This is guided by the following questions:

☐ Which functions and activities are absolutely necessary if the organization is to thrive?

☐ Are there alternative ways in which given functions can be performed with greater efficiency and effectiveness?

☐ What new skills and functions are needed to enhance overall productivity?

☐ Are compensation levels geared to reality?

A detailed answer to each of these issues would take us well beyond the scope of this book. It is more helpful to briefly discuss four distinct ways in which restructuring can take place, each of which can offer genuine benefits in terms of reduction of unneeded functions and services, greater operating efficiency and enhanced field effectiveness.

Downsizing. Few agencies can afford the luxury of a large headquarters staff and layers of accountability. The move toward greater field autonomy eliminates many service functions, thus requiring downsizing. Furthermore, entire units or programs may be dropped on the basis of diminished need.

Field alliances. Others will be challenged to join the growing trend toward cooperative field relationships based on a common vision and the contribution of different roles from cooperating parties. The potential benefits are many, but these can be gained only by a willingness to sacrifice autonomy and power.[18]

Establishment of specialized entities. It may be necessary to establish separate but cooperating "niche" agencies. This facilitates a move from being a generalist to concentrating on a few things that can make the greatest contribution. Large, general-purpose agencies will likely face peril unless such steps are courageously taken.

Local church/agency alliances. The unmistakable trend toward missions-minded churches assuming agency roles can become a real advantage in advancing the kingdom. Growing numbers of churches are actively seeking agency help as they become more proactive. Others welcome field partnerships by churches and agencies. The latter development is especially welcome, because the church contributes its resources and its zeal in fresh recognition that God is a missionary God, whereas the agency brings experience and expertise. This form of restructuring alliances is certain to grow.

Putting It All Together

Bud Anderson has assumed the challenge of his career by turning GHM in directions that can bring about genuine transformation. Bud and his team, however, must face the brutal truth that only about 15 percent of business enterprises successfully complete a full-scale transformation process.[19] Nonetheless, most who are genuinely committed to change make enough progress to achieve a noticeable difference.

It is entirely likely this transformation will require many carefully conceived steps over an extended period of time. There will be setbacks and frustrations along the way. But one thing is certain— *GHM will either become a very different agency over time, or it will be mired in obsolescence.*

The biggest obstacle that GHM will encounter is of course the old nemesis: it is human nature to resist change. It is far easier to stay within our theological and managerial ruts than to break out in new directions. One of the most important steps that Bud can take to counter this resistance is to make sure that the vision produces short-term results. This is done through breaking change down into bite-size stages, each of which represents a significant forward step.

One example might be the launch of a new on-field leadership development program, starting with hands-on instruction on how to undertake an outcomes assessment. Once this is done, a celebration is held by the board and leadership to acknowledge a genuine victory over an obstacle to transformation. Full credit is given to those who make it a reality, thus motivating others to become involved in further steps forward.

We applaud the leadership teams and boards of agencies who are beginning to embrace the transformation process. It requires courage and unwavering trust that Jesus will faithfully make his presence known as Lord of all that takes place. His lordship offers assurance that the birth pains will be rewarded by a revived spiritual vitality and ministry effectiveness.

7

....

Missions in a
Postmodern
World
Will the Clouds Lift?

*Over two thousand years ago our God, a missionary God, sent his
Son, who devoted his life to building a church that would with-
stand the very gates of hell. The mission Jesus gave to his disciples is as real today as it was in their time—Follow my teaching
and my example, extend my spiritual kingdom on this earth by
making disciples among all peoples starting right here and
moving beyond to the very ends of the world. As you do this, I
will be with you, giving you the power to do greater things
together than I ever could in my few short years. Rejoice and
follow me!*

*   *   *

TODAY THERE IS A WORLDWIDE CHRISTIAN PRESENCE THAT FEW
ever could have anticipated at the start of the modern missions
movement in the early 1800s. Yet as we have endeavored to point
out in these pages, something has gone wrong with the harvest.

Somehow the commission the Lord left has become distorted and even corrupted in Christian outlook and ministry since the middle of the nineteenth century.

This book was written to join with a number of other voices[1] in calling the church back to biblical fidelity and wisdom. Some might object that we have said little that is new. Our response is simply *if this is the case, what is holding us back from responding as we should?* It is our prayer that our words here will be used by God as a call for action. It is time to break out of our captivity to modernity!

Responding to a Postmodern World

Our basic concerns with the prevailing practice of world missions today fall broadly into two categories, one historical and the other biblical.

A captivity to modernity. Western missions theology and practice has fallen captive to modernity—a pattern of thinking that has been especially prevalent in America for almost two hundred years. This has led to an outlook that envisions world missions as a movement from a political and economic power center outward toward a poor and needy periphery, which is viewed as "the mission field."

Modernity further shaped the traditional paradigm of world missions through its predominant characteristics of volunteerism and individualism. As a result, religious belief has come to be perceived and practiced as little more than a private and personal affair in isolation from the larger public and social world. To make matters worse, the Western missionary outlook and practice has been infused with rationalism—a pattern of pragmatic and managerially motivated reasoning through which methods and techniques have come to drive both missions theology and strategy in many circles.

We do not deny that this way of thinking has accomplished much throughout the world, especially in areas where Western political power has been in the ascendancy. Our contention, however, is that we have entered a postmodern world where these patterns of thought and action are becoming positively harmful. Postmodernism is a decided pendulum swing in a more healthy direction, and to the surprise of many it is bringing us closer in many ways to the traditional and still prevalent outlooks in much of the Two-Thirds World as well as to the times in which Jesus lived and ministered:[2]

1. *The legitimacy of human values, including religious belief, has been restored as an essential element alongside rationality.* In other words, religion no longer is considered, especially among today's student generation, to be myth. Therefore, the artificial gap between the so-called private and public worlds has been removed, and religious values now are increasingly seen as pertinent for all of life.

2. *The ever-present reality of evil has significantly undercut the optimistic notion that all human problems are solvable.*

3. *Individuality is yielding to community as the essential means of coping with life.*

4. *The church has responded positively to the breadth and depth of biblical thinking about God as a missionary God.* Equally critical as its captivity to modernity was that missions strategy lost sight of the breadth and depth of biblical thinking about God's purposes for his creation. What does it mean for missions that God has displayed his dynamic and loving initiative in creation and in the incarnation of Christ? It means that *missions is primarily God's work* and that we, God's people, in obedience to the leading of the Holy Spirit come alongside and join him where he is at work. The initiative and direction comes from God, not from ourselves.

World missions grows out of God's own trinitarian reality as this is revealed in the great story of redemption. The story focuses on Jesus Christ, who by the will of the Father, inaugurated a new order of creation through his life, death and resurrection. We have the wonderful opportunity to participate in this new order by the empowering of the Holy Spirit.

The fourfold account of Christ's Great Commission in the Gospels reveals that missions flowing from this new reality is holistic, centered in the reign of Christ and seeks the physical and spiritual health of all people in their cultures and communities. Missions brings justice at the same time as it offers mercy.

Furthermore, missions is communal in that it grows out of and issues in the growth of the body of Christ, the church, which is both the medium and the message that reveals and interprets the power of God's word for the world. The church is missionary by its very nature (1 Pet 2:9). It is on a pilgrimage as it is called out of the world and sent back, not to proclaim a system of beliefs but to issue a call to *follow Jesus* and to discover *together* that he is the way, the truth and the life.

New realities in world missions. These historical and theological concerns are compounded by the reality at the dawn of the third millennium that God has raised up a mighty body of believers in the younger churches who are eagerly carrying the message of salvation around the world—even back to our Western nations. Through God's grace these non-Western churches have attained maturity and vitality and have been placed at the forefront of his activity in contemporary history. It cannot be denied that the initiative for world missions today is carried more often by pentecostal churches in Latin America or independent churches in Africa than by North American or European agencies.

This new missions force, by and large, has the courage to break out of modernity's trap and foresake strategies that were duly taught to them by their Western missionary forefathers. The reality is that we in the West are now in the position of becoming learners rather than teachers; partners rather than leaders.

An Agenda for a Gracious Revolution

We are united in the conviction that the opportunities for growth of Christ's spiritual kingdom worldwide have never been greater. For this to happen, however, there must be a gracious revolution.[3] Mission, Inc., must embrace the biblical pattern in which God's Word often spreads from the periphery to the center.

This revolution can take place through an unprecedented collaborative effort in which North American missions play an important but not dominant role of enhancing the initiatives of others, serving as one among many in partnerships and alliances. In so doing we honor God's intent that his gospel spread to the ends of the earth from a united body through "mutual exchange of gifts between multiple and complementary centers of missionary influence," as we stated thoughout this book.

We have taken you on a journey into some uncharted waters with First Church of Rollingwood and Global Harvest Mission. The interlocking stories of two fictitious but representative entities began with a decisive break from modernity. In no small part this was due to their recognizing that much of what is wrong in world missions is due to our abstracting the Great Commission from the full counsel of God's Word.

We hope you have received encouragement and insight from their experiences. While each has embarked on a long and uncertain journey, *they are moving in the right direction.* Both groups welcomed a fresh vision of the all-encompassing reign of Christ, with mature disciples following his lead in his spiritual kingdom through a church that is a beacon light of his living reality.

Pastor Geoff Finch and his leadership team at First Church clearly heard the prompting of God. They took the first steps by stripping away the entrapments of institutionalism. They focused anew on releasing the people and resources of First Church so it can function as the living organism, as its missionary God intends.

Bud Anderson, on the other hand, responded by launching an organizational transformation at GHM. The challenge he faced with a courageous board and leadership team was to cast off a Western cultural captivity that had come to envision world missions as a conversion-focused, managerial task. GHM also was thrust into a fresh new recognition that ministry to the world must be motivated by a vision of the reign of Christ and ministry to the center from the periphery, from many centers of influence to new unreached areas.

In the transformation process the local church was restored by this agency to its rightful position at one of the multiple centers of world missions, and GHM ventured forth into a largely unknown world of cooperation and partnership. Fresh insights also emerged on how to discern and respond strategically to the voice of the Holy Spirit through field alliances and partnerships working to establish, strengthen and extend points of light throughout the world.

This book has not been an easy one to write. Both of us have been forced to come to grips with the sobering recognition that much of our own ministry and outlook has been contaminated by modern practices. How can we point fingers of blame at others? One thing is for sure—we are all the more amazed that God continues to work through disciples who persist in grasping his purposes so dimly and following his lead so poorly. He continues to build his church through us but also in spite of us. We can only raise our voices in praise to say, "All glory to the King of Kings."

Our plea to each reader is simply this: let us together put aside all that we assumed to be biblical and missiological sophistication and join together in a gracious revolution as pilgrims venturing forth on an uncertain journey with only a dim vision of the road ahead. Here are a few foundational principles that may shed some light as we venture forth together and that might guide missions thinking and planning in the emerging world situation. No one, least of all this author team, can foresee the future with any degree of clarity. Nonetheless, we can extend and extrapolate some qualities and characteristics, most of which are already present on the horizon.

1. *The kingdom and reign of Christ will be extended primarily through localized initiatives that infiltrate all segments of society.* World missions has all too often assumed the characteristics of a mass-marketing campaign undertaken in response to seemingly endless calls to "finish the task." Our contention is that this often disregards the fact, first of all, that the reign of Christ grows as a mustard seed, one person at a time, one community at a time. While large-scale initiatives have their place, they should be the outgrowth of collaborative efforts that build upon and amplify what already has been established locally.

2. *The local church will be restored to its central role in the reign of Christ.* The local church will once again be affirmed as God's chosen means for spreading the gospel through ministry that radiates outward and multiplies from these cells of the kingdom. World missions will focus on ongoing initiatives to plant and build churches that model and proclaim the good news through their words (1 Pet 3:15) and their lifestyle of personal holiness, which exemplifies Jesus Christ. This will take place only when churches are conceived as an organism built around community, which provides a genuine witness to a living Christ and is an authentic and appealing option to

those living by the standards of the world (Eph 5:1-21).

3. *There will be no dichotomy between evangelism and social transformation.* Evangelism will once again be viewed as only the first step in an ongoing process of reaching the lost and making disciples through baptizing all who respond, teaching them to "produce fruit in keeping with repentance" (Mt 3:8; 28:18-20). It will no longer be seen as a methodology but will be embraced as the outcome of a lifestyle centered in true empathy based on love, genuine respect and willingness to address the deepest longings of others with the good news of Jesus (1 Pet 3:15).

Social justice and ecological responsibility also will be restored to their proper place in Christian witness. Throughout this book we have emphasized the holistic nature of the gospel, which recognizes that God is interested in the whole of life, our bodies as well as our spirits, individuals and families, as well as communities and nations. Furthermore, God also cares about his creation and expects his people to be responsible stewards. Having said this, however, we recognize the legitimacy of initiatives that specialize in just one part of the total responsibility God has given us. This is all the more reason for alliances and partnerships where, together, specialized entities are part of the ministry of God in all of its aspects.

4. *There will be obedience to the entirety of Christ's Great Commission.* The objective of world missions will move beyond conversion, the essential first step, to making disciples who are equipped to follow their Lord and Master. Everything possible will be done to equip mature believers and unleash them for responsible ministry. For this to happen, renewed emphasis will be placed on equipping servant leaders through intentional leadership development to follow the model of Jesus with his disciples.

5. *We will learn from the temptations of Jesus.* Jesus at the outset of his ministry was forced to contend with three of the most powerful temptations Satan could offer—expediency, popularity and power (Mt 4:1-11). It would have been expedient, logical and even strategic for Jesus to have ended his forty-day fast by turning stones into bread. He could have attracted the attention, interest and admiration of an entire nation had he leaped from the top of the temple and

landed on his feet. Most of all, he could have ruled over all of the earth if he had just bowed down to Satan.

Think of it—Satan offered Jesus the opportunity to complete all he came to earth to accomplish—in one stroke he would rule the world. Would something like this be a temptation to Mission, Inc.? At long last the Great Commission could be fulfilled in our generation by our efforts and ingenuity. Jesus had a very different agenda, however. His was to be a spiritual kingdom based on unwavering obedience to all that he had learned from his Father. He engaged in no sloganeering to "complete the task," no triumphalistic Great Commission countdowns, no strategic plan and timetable other than the certainty that he would be forsaken by his followers and left to experience a traumatic, lonely death.

We suggest that those of us on this missions pilgrimage reexamine our rhetoric and publicity. Let us join in the sober recognition that the spiritual kingdom of Jesus is distinctly and irreversibly countercultural. It is all about communities witnessing to Christ's kingdom without the convictions of worldly expediency, glamour and power. Yet without fanfare it transforms the world.

We would not deny the assistance of today's technology along this journey. But it is not the strategic means by which we reach the goal—it is simply a resource and nothing more. We will need to think strategically as we reach intersections in the road, but this is always undergirded by the countercultural practice of prayer and fasting, even in the midst of our sometimes wavering human confidence that the Lord will accomplish his purposes if we only follow him in obedience and humility. In short, a quiet, gentle revolution.

6. *Missions will be responsive to God's initiatives in the world.* World missions belongs to God, not to us. He alone is the divine planner. At best we will only weakly grasp his strategy, regardless of our own strategic sophistication. Therefore, our only option is to ask God, *What do you want us to do?* We have access to almost limitless computerized data banks that reveal human needs of overwhelming magnitude. But *the existence of need or even opportunity does not represent call.* Our task is to discern where God is at work and seek to discover our part in the divine mosaic.

One of our major contentions has been that cultural changes associated with postmodernity offer unusual opportunities as well as challenges for Christian missions. Old political and economic centers of influence are being challenged. Centralized and unified patterns of thinking and planning are no longer accepted without question. And for emerging young leaders, there is evidence that a genuine missionary lifestyle can take shape, even as they move through various stages in their career (which according to recent studies may traverse an average of six different jobs). Understanding and engaging these changes is how we respond to what God is doing in the world. Careful, sensitive, prayerful response to a changing world is all part of our obedience to the fullness of Christ's commission. God may sometimes use the recognized leaders of this world. But he delights in working through ordinary people committed to communal discernment and prayer.

7. *There will be a restored understanding of God's people as colaborers, created by him to carry out his work through strategic thinking.* In recognition that God alone must take the strategic initiative, the people of God will assume enlightened responsibility for stewardship that is ensured by strategic thinking, proper management of resources and ongoing evaluation. Strategic thinking is a valid endeavor for Christians. It is a corporate process that takes human initiative and rational processes seriously. Nevertheless, it is to be activated and empowered only through divine counsel. In other words, we respond to the call and leading of God. Rational thinking is infused with prayer and scriptural reflection. Even then there is no certainty—we venture forth on a pilgrimage, seeking the best options, learning as we go, turning and adapting where we must.

We must recognize that ministry outcomes are entirely a testimony to the glory of God, not a tribute to human strategic wisdom. Some of today's popular missiological rhetoric smacks of self-assured strategic infallibility. What is our intent? To glorify ourselves or to glorify God?

8. *Strategic ministry will be undertaken when it is demonstrated to foster partnership and collaboration.* There are mission "lone wolves" in every field, especially from independent churches, who often ven-

ture out with little counsel and experience, radiating an unwarranted confidence and sense of superiority. When venturing into a new work we must take time to discern who already is engaged there or is contemplating a particular step. Then we can determine what role we might play there.

Now is the time to establish alliances that cross international borders so that kingdom resources may be combined and mobilized as mutual centers of influence. Remember Paul's counsel that the gifts given to various members of the body are given for the building up of the whole body "until we all reach unity in the faith and in the knowledge of the Son of God and become mature, attaining to the whole measure of the fullness of Christ" (Eph 4:13). We are inextricably bound together in this great reality called the body of Christ. And God can use every single part of it.

A corollary principle follows from what we have just said: any initiative that fosters competition or ignores what other Christians have done or intend to do cannot expect God's blessing. We are particularly distressed by missions outreaches motivated by a desire to plant a denominational church simply because that denomination does not have a presence in a particular geographic location. God's work has nothing to do with denominational priorities based on assumed superiority. What a difference it makes when a deliberate effort is made to develop a collaborative relationship that offers the best opportunity to steward the gifts of the entire body of Christ!

Guiding Criteria for Ministry in a Postmodern World

Let us summarize what we have tried to say in the form of a series of questions. We pray these will help shed light on the path of all who follow our Lord in the pilgrimage of world missions.

1. Does the proposed strategy enhance localized efforts and initiatives that infiltrate all segments of society?

2. Will local churches in both the sending country and the field of ministry assume their central role in the world mission of Jesus Christ?

3. Does the envisioned strategy encompass the full gospel of the kingdom in which there is no dichotomy between evangelism and

social transformation?

4. Is the strategy based on the totality of the Great Commission, so that disciples are taught and motivated to follow all that Christ modeled and proclaimed?

5. Is the strategy grounded in prayer and fasting, seeking the will of God as he reveals where he wants us to join him in his work in the world?

6. Is proper stewardship being demonstrated by strategic thinking undertaken in a commitment to be true colaborers with God?

7. Does the initiative foster collaboration and partnership?

Come Lord Jesus

It is a formidable challenge to return to missions theology and strategy that breaks out of modernity and centers anew on all that Jesus taught about his kingdom and his reign. God's call is a communal one, and its fruit may go largely unnoticed in the power centers of the world. It is unquestionably countercultural and subversive in its opposition to the self-seeking power plays that today's world enthrones as good and worthy.

Yet the good news of the kingdom continues to quietly transform lives and communities. Indeed it points not just to a better world but to a whole new creation that Christ will one day unveil. Toward that day we work, and for that day we pray: even so, *come Lord Jesus*.

Notes

Chapter 1: A Clouded Future?

[1]Some readers will recognize this scenario as having first appeared in a monograph written for mission agency leaders a few years ago. It has been modified, however, and updated with permission of the publisher. See James F. Engel, *Clouded Future? Advancing North American World Missions* (Milwaukee: Christian Stewardship Association, 1996), pp. 1-2.

[2]See Paul McKaughan, Dellanna O'Brien and William O'Brien, *Choosing a Future for U.S. Missions* (Monrovia, Calif.: MARC Publications, 1998).

[3]Engel, *Clouded Future?* p. 4.

[4]John Ronsvalle and Sylvia Ronsvalle, *Behind the Stained Glass Windows: Money Dynamics in the Church* (Grand Rapids, Mich.: Baker, 1996).

[5]See James F. Engel and Jerry Jones, *Baby Boomers and the Future of World Missions* (Orange, Calif.: Management Development Associates, 1989).

[6]Engel, *Clouded Future?* chap. 5.

[7]David B. Barrett and Todd M. Johnson, "Annual Statistical Table on Global Mission: 1988," *International Bulletin of Missionary Research* 22 (January 1998): 27.

[8]Dallas Willard, *The Spirit of the Disciplines* (San Francisco: Harper, 1988), p. 23.

[9]Mark Noll, *The Scandal of the Evangelical Mind* (Grand Rapids, Mich.: Eerdmans, 1994).

[10]Tokunboh Adeyemo, "The Lessons of Rwanda for the Church in Africa," *World Pulse* 31 (December 20, 1996): 5.

[11]This prayer was first stated in James F. Engel, *The Peril of Outmoded Paradigms for World Evangelization* (Colorado Springs: Development Associates International, 1998), p. 25.

Chapter 2: Where in the World Is Jerusalem?

[1]David J. Bosch, *Transforming Mission* (Maryknoll, N.Y.: Orbis, 1991), p. 519.

[2]See Earle E. Cairns, *An Endless Line of Splendors: Revivals and Their Leaders from the Great Awakening to the Present* (Wheaton, Ill.: Tyndale House,

1986).

[3]Donald Hagner, *Commentary on Matthew* (Waco, Tex.: Word, 1996), 2:887.

[4]See Richard Peace, *Conversion in the New Testament* (Grand Rapids, Mich.: Eerdmans, 1999).

[5]Scholars disagree about who wrote the ending that appears in brackets in most Bibles. Some believe that it is Marcan, but all agree that the ideas in the ending are consistent with those found elsewhere in Mark.

[6]Craig S. Keener, *The IVP Bible Background Commentary: New Testament* (Downers Grove, Ill.: InterVarsity Press, 1993), p. 319.

[7]This idea is further developed in William Dyrness, *The Earth Is God's* (Maryknoll, N.Y.: Orbis, 1997), pp. 114-24.

[8]Bosch, *Transforming Mission*, pp. 389-90.

[9]Ferdinand Hahn, *Mission in the New Testament*, Studies in Biblical Theology 47 (London: SCM Press, 1965), p. 10.

[10]Joachim Jeremias, *Jesus' Promise to the Nations*, Studies in Biblical Theology 24 (London: SCM Press, 1967), p. 9.

[11]See Hahn, *Mission in the New Testament*, p. 10.

[12]Roland Allen, who anticipated much of our argument ninety years ago, pointed out that while Paul did not deliberately aim at any class, most people in his audience were from the lower commercial classes (Roland Allen, *Missionary Methods: St. Paul's or Ours?* 2nd ed. [Grand Rapids, Mich.: Eerdmans, 1962], p. 24). Rodney Stark, however, has recently argued that the makeup of the early church was fairly representative of the Roman Empire. See Rodney Stark, *The Rise of Christianity* (Princeton, N.J.: Princeton University Press, 1996).

[13]See Keith F. Nickle, *The Collection: A Study in Paul's Strategy*, Studies in Biblical Theology 48 (Naperville, Ill.: Allensson, 1966), pp. 100-130. Nickle points out that the closest parallel is that of the temple tax sent from dispersed Jews to Jerusalem. Hence Paul may be implying that this is the new temple of God conducting its services (Eph 2:21).

[14]See the argument of Paul Barnett, *Jesus and the Rise of Early Christianity* (Downers Grove, Ill.: InterVarsity Press, 1999), pp. 328-53.

[15]See Jonathan Bonk, "All Things to All Persons: Missionary as a Racist-Imperialist," *Missiology* 8, no. 3 (1980): 285-306.

[16]Lamin Sanneh, "Mission and the Modern Imperative," in *Earthen Vessels: American Evangelicals and Foreign Missions*, ed. Joel Carpenter and Wilbert Shenk (Grand Rapids, Mich.: Eerdmans, 1990), p. 301.

[17]Vinay Samuel and Chris Sugden, eds., *Sharing Jesus in the Two Thirds World* (Grand Rapids, Mich.: Eerdmans, 1983), pp. 6-7.

[18]See on this point Peter van Roeden, "Nineteenth Century Representations

of Missionary Conversion and the Transformation of Western Christianity," in *Conversion to Modernities: The Globalization of Christianity*, ed. Peter van der Veer (New York: Routledge and Kegan Paul, 1996), pp. 65-84. And for the values that lie behind this, see Nathan Hatch, *The Democratization of American Religion* (New Haven, Conn.: Yale University Press, 1989).

[19]Andrew W. Walls, *The Missionary Movement in Christian History: Studies in the Transmission of Faith* (Maryknoll, N.Y.: Orbis, 1996), p. 237.

[20]See the news story "African Missionaries to the U.S.," *Christian Century*, August 13-20, 1997, pp. 718-20, quote from p. 718. Figures are from Patrick Johnston, *Operation World*, quoted in this article.

[21]The source of our knowledge was a prayer letter from the Filipino president of the Asian Theological Seminary in Manila, Dr. Isabelo F. Magalit, who was one of the expositors at the conference, dated October 15, 1997.

[22]Joel Carpenter and Wilber Shenk, ed., *Earthen Vessels* (Ann Arbor, Mich.: Demand, 1990), p. 316.

[23]Paul Hawken, *The Ecology of Commerce: A Declaration of Sustainability* (New York: Harper Business, 1993), p. 93. He is referring to the work of Richard O'Brien, *The End of Geography*.

[24]Walls, *Missionary Movement*, pp. 258-59.

[25]See R. G. Robins, "Azusa Street Mission" in *Dictionary of Christianity in America*, ed. Daniel G. Reid et al. (Downers Grove, Ill.: InterVarsity Press, 1990), and the bibliography noted there.

[26]In Paul E. Pretiz and W. Dayton Roberts, "Uncharted Waters: The Evolution of a Mission," *The Story of the Community of Latin American Ministries* (San Jose, Costa Rica: CLAME, 1997), p. 35.

[27]Ibid., p. 25.

[28]Vinoth Ramachandra, *Gods That Fail* (Downers Grove, Ill.: InterVarsity Press, 1996), p. 219.

Chapter 3: What's Gone Wrong with the Harvest?

[1]Bob Fryling, quoted in Brian D. McLaren, *Reinventing Your Church* (Grand Rapids, Mich.: Zondervan, 1998), pp. 165-87.

[2]McLaren, *Reinventing Your Church*. See also Brian Walsh and Richard Middleton, *Truth Is Stranger Than It Used to Be* (Downers Grove, Ill.: InterVarsity Press, 1996).

[3]Os Guinness, "Mission in the Face of Modernity," a paper presented at Lausanne II, an international congress on world evangelization, in Manila, 1989. The paper was published in abstracted form in *Proclaim Christ Until He Comes*, ed. J. D. Douglas (Minneapolis: World Wide Publications, 1990), pp. 283-88, and in *Faith and Modernity*, ed. Philip Sampson (Oxford: Reg-

num-Lynx, 1994).

⁴A useful source on the roots of modernism is Lesslie Newbigin, *Truth and Authority in Modernity* (Valley Forge, Penn.: Trinity Press International, 1996).

⁵Lesslie Newbigin, "Knowing and Believing," in *The Gospel in a Pluralistic Society* (Grand Rapids, Mich.: Eerdmans, 1989).

⁶See Bruce Bradshaw, *Bridging the Gap* (Monrovia, Calif.: MARC Publications, 1993), p. 30.

⁷Mark Noll, *The Scandal of the Evangelical Mind* (Grand Rapids, Mich.: Eerdmans, 1994), chap. 6.

⁸Ibid., p. 42.

⁹See the classic study by Timothy L. Smith, *Revivalism and Social Reform in Mid-Nineteenth Century America* (New York: Abingdon, 1957). Also see Joel A. Carpenter, "Revivalism Without Social Reform," *Books & Culture*, November-December 1998, pp. 26-29, regarding changes after 1860. See also Earle E. Cairns, *An Endless Line of Splendors: Revivals and Their Leaders from the Great Awakening to the Present* (Wheaton, Ill.: Tyndale House, 1986).

¹⁰See Cairns, *Endless Line of Splendors*, chap. 10.

¹¹William A. Dyrness, *How Does America Hear the Gospel?* (Grand Rapids, Mich.: Eerdmans, 1989), pp. 32-37.

¹²Noll, *Scandal of the Evangelical Mind*, p. 120.

¹³David J. Bosch, *Transforming Mission* (Maryknoll, N.Y.: Orbis, 1991), p. 318, emphasis added.

¹⁴Os Guinness, *The Gravedigger File* (Downers Grove, Ill.: InterVarsity Press, 1983), p. 80, emphasis added.

¹⁵John Wesley, as quoted in Howard A Snyder, *The Radical Wesley* (Downers Grove, Ill.: InterVarsity Press, 1980), p. 85.

¹⁶Newbigin, *Gospel in a Pluralistic Society*, p. 133.

¹⁷Dallas Willard, *The Spirit of the Disciplines* (San Francisco: Harper, 1988), p. 15.

¹⁸Ibid., p. 23.

¹⁹The discussion here closely follows James F. Engel, *The Peril of Outmoded Paradigms for World Evangelization* (Colorado Springs: Development Associates International, 1998), pp. 10-28.

²⁰John Seel, "Modernity and Evangelicals," in *Faith and Modernity*, ed. P. Sampson, Vinay Samuel and Christopher Sugden (Oxford: Regnum-Lynx, 1994), p. 291.

²¹Paul McKaughan, Dellanna O'Brien and William O'Brien, *Choosing a Future for U.S. Missions* (Monrovia, Calif.: MARC Publications, 1998), pp. 23-24.

[22]Seel, "Modernity and Evangelicals," p. 308.

[23]Dyrness, *How Does America Hear the Gospel?* chap. 3.

[24]Samuel Escobar, "A Movement Divided," *Transformation,* October 1991, p. 9.

[25]James F. Engel, "The Great Commission Advertising Campaign: Misuse of the Media in World Evangelization," *Transformation,* October 1993, pp. 21-23.

[26]James F. Engel, "The Road to Conversion: The Latest Research Insights," *Evangelical Missions Quarterly,* April 1990, pp. 185-93.

[27]John R. W. Stott, *Christian Mission in the Modern World* (Downers Grove, Ill.: InterVarsity Press, 1976), p. 127.

[28]Donald A. McGavran, *Understanding Church Growth* (Grand Rapids, Mich.: Eerdmans, 1980), p. 24.

[29]For an insightful empirical analysis of this principle see Christian A. Schwarz, *Natural Church Development* (Emmelsbull, Germany: Verlags, 1996).

[30]Orlando Costas, *The Church and Its Mission: A Shattering Critique from the Third World* (Wheaton, Ill.: Tyndale House, 1974), p. 76.

[31]Engel, "Road to Conversion," pp. 185-93.

[32]Glenn Schwartz, "It's Time to Get Serious About the Cycle of Dependency in Africa," *Mission Frontiers,* January-February 1997, pp. 8-14.

[33]Alex de Waal, *Famine Crimes: Politics and the Disaster Relief Industry in Africa* (Bloomington: Indiana University Press, 1997), pp. 138-40.

[34]See Lesslie Newbigin, *Foolishness to the Greeks: The Gospel and Western Culture* (Grand Rapids, Mich.: Eerdmans, 1986), and his *Gospel in a Pluralistic Society.* For his influence in the United States, see George R. Hunsberger and Craig Van Gelder, eds., *The Church Between Gospel and Culture* (Grand Rapids, Mich.: Eerdmans, 1996).

[35]Joel Carpenter, *Revive Us Again* (New York: Oxford University Press, 1997), pp. 28-30.

[36]Bruce Camp, "Paradigm Shifts in World Evangelization," *Mobilizer,* winter 1994, pp. 1-16.

[37]David B. Barrett and James W. Reapsome, *Seven Hundred Plans to Evangelize the World: The Rise of a Global Evangelization Movement* (Birmingham, Ala.: New Hope, 1988).

[38]Noll, *Scandal of the Evangelical Mind,* p. 107.

Chapter 4: Missions in a Postmodern World: A Gracious Revolution

[1]Philip Yancey, *What's So Amazing About Grace?* (Grand Rapids, Mich.: Zondervan, 1997), chap. 19.

[2]James Plueddemann, "SIM's Agenda for a Gracious Revolution," *International Bulletin of Missionary Research* 23 (1999): 156-60.

[3]This was first published in James F. Engel, *The Peril of Outmoded Paradigms for World Mission* (Colorado Springs: Development Associates International, 1998).

[4]This term is attributed to our friend and colleague Samuel Escobar. See "A Movement Divided," *Transformation,* October 1991, pp. 7-12.

[5]See David B. Barrett and Todd M. Johnson, "Annual Statistical Table on Global Mission: 1999," *International Bulletin of Missionary Research,* January 1999, p. 25.

[6]Plueddemann, "SIM's Agenda."

[7]Henry T. Blackaby and Claude V. King, *Experiencing God* (Fort Worth, Tex.: Broadman & Holman, 1994), p. 32.

[8]Ibid., pp. 253-54.

[9]Ron Sider, "What Is the Gospel?" *Transformation,* January-March 1999, p. 31.

[10]Os Guinness, *The Gravedigger File* (Downers Grove, Ill.: InterVarsity, 1983), p. 80.

[11]Peter Kuzmič, "Twelve Theses on Kingdom Servanthood for Post-Communist Europe," *Transformation,* January-March 1999, p. 37.

[12]Kathryn T. Long, *The Revival of 1857-1858: Interpreting an American Religious Awakening* (London: Oxford University Press, 1997).

[13]Bruce Bradshaw, *Bridging the Gap* (Monrovia, Calif.: MARC Publications, 1993), p. 17.

[14]Valdir R. Steuernagel, "Social Concern and Evangelization: Our Journey Since Lausanne," *Transformation,* January-March 1990, pp. 12-16.

[15]John R. W. Stott, "Twenty Years After Lausanne: Some Personal Reflections," *International Bulletin of Missionary Research,* April 1995, p. 54.

[16]We gratefully acknowledge the insights of our friend the late Orlando E. Costas in an unpublished paper entitled "Christian World Mission in a Galilean Perspective." This paper crystallized and clarified thinking that had previously appeared in two important books. See especially Orlando Costas, *The Church and Its Mission: A Shattering Critique from the Third World* (Wheaton, Ill.: Tyndale House, 1974), and his *The Integrity of Mission* (New York: Harper & Row, 1979).

[17]Wendy M. Zoba, "The Gypsy Reformation," *Christianity Today,* February 8, 1999, pp. 51-54.

[18]For a discussion of some early attempts to learn from these other voices, see William Dyrness, *Learning About Theology from the Third World* (Grand Rapids, Mich.: Zondervan, 1990).

[19]Here we signal the exception of Phill Butler and Interdev, which includes development of strategic partnerships in its core mission.

[20]Plueddemann, "SIM's Agenda."

[21]Blackaby and King, *Experiencing God*, pp. 138, 140.

[22]For an insightful contemporary interpretation of *Pilgrim's Progress*, see Brent Curtis and John Eldridge, *The Sacred Romance* (Nashville: Nelson, 1997).

[23]James F. Engel, "The Great Commission Advertising Campaign: Misuse of the Media in World Evangelization," *Transformation*, October 1993, pp. 21-23.

[24]This was first published in two slightly different versions. See James F. Engel, "The Audience for Christian Communication," in *Let the Earth Hear His Voice*, ed. J. D. Douglas (Minneapolis: World Wide Publications, 1975), pp. 535-39. Also Viggo B. Sogaard, *Everything You Need to Know for a Cassette Ministry* (Minneapolis: Bethany Fellowship, 1975).

[25]Allen Swanson, "Decisions or Disciples? A Study of Evangelism Effectiveness in Taiwan," *Missiology*, January 1989, pp. 54-67.

[26]Avery Dulles, *Models of the Church* (Garden City, N.Y.: Doubleday, 1974), p. 32.

[27]Lesslie Newbigin, *The Gospel in a Pluralistic Society* (Grand Rapids, Mich.: Eerdmans, 1989), chap. 18.

[28]Rick Warren, *The Purpose-Driven Church* (Grand Rapids, Mich.: Zondervan, 1996), p. 5, emphasis added.

[29]Vinay Samuel, "Evangelical Response to Globalization: An Asian Perspective," *Transformation*, January-March 1999, p. 7.

Chapter 5: The Church in Missions

[1]Darrel Guder, ed., *Missional Church: A Vision for the Sending of the Church in North America* (Grand Rapids, Mich.: Eerdmans, 1998), p. 54. See also Wade Clark Roof and William McKinney, *American Mainline Religion: Its Changing Shape and Future* (New Brunswick, N.J.: Rutgers University Press, 1987).

[2]George Barna, *Today's Pastor: A Revealing Look at What Pastors Are Saying About Themselves, Their Peers and the Pressures They Face* (Ventura, Calif.: Regal, 1993), p. 50.

[3]These data are reported in the *Los Angeles Times*, September 4, 1998, sec. A, pp. 1, 32-33. See also Wade Clark Roof, *A Generation of Seekers* (San Francisco: HarperSanFrancisco, 1993).

[4]Guder, *Missional Church*, pp. 79ff.

[5]This is the argument in Robert Wuthnow, *Communities of Discourse* (Cam-

bridge: Harvard University Press, 1989), pt 1.

[6]Jacques Ellul, *The Technological Society* (New York: Alfred A. Knopf, 1964).

[7]In fact Rodney Stark has recently argued that it was this mutual caring that proved so persuasive to outsiders and became one of the primary reasons for the rapid growth of the church in the first three hundred years. See Stark, *The Rise of Christianity* (Princeton, N.J.: Princeton University Press, 1996).

[8]C. S. Lewis, *Letters to Malcolm: Chiefly on Prayer*, quoted (unattributed) in *Radix* 26, no. 2 (1998): 3.

[9]There are helpful books on this subject. We especially recommend Brian McLaren, *Reinventing Your Church* (Grand Rapids, Mich.: Zondervan, 1998); and Rick Warren, *The Purpose-Driven Church* (Grand Rapids, Mich.: Zondervan, 1995).

[10]This is the ministry statement of Church of the Open Door in Crystal, Minnesota, a suburb of Minneapolis. It is used with the permission of missions pastor Steve Hanson.

[11]See James F. Engel, *Clouded Future? Advancing North American World Missions* (Milwaukee: Christian Stewardship Association, 1996).

[12]McLaren, *Reinventing Your Church*, p. 143.

[13]See Donald E. Miller, *Reinventing American Protestantism: Christianity in the New Millennium* (Berkeley: University of California, 1998). Miller is currently engaged in similar research in large cities in the Two-Thirds World and finding surprising similarities.

Chapter 6: The Missions Agency

[1]Bill Ogden, "Reshaping Missions for the 21st Century" (unpublished paper, South America Mission).

[2]Ralph Winter, "Countdown 2000!" *World Evangelization*, November-December 1988.

[3]Ralph Winter, "Editorial," *Mission Frontiers*, January-February 1995, p. 4.

[4]James F. Engel, *Clouded Future? Advancing North American World Missions* (Milwaukee: Christian Stewardship Association, 1996), p. 120.

[5]Peter Drucker, *The New Realities* (New York: Harper & Row, 1989).

[6]Tom Peters, *Liberation Management* (New York: Fauwcett Columbine, 1992).

[7]Peter Senge, *The Fifth Discipline* (New York: Doubleday Currency, 1990).

[8]John P. Kotter, "Winning at Change," *Leader to Leader*, fall 1998, p. 32.

[9]Ibid., p. 28.

[10]James Plueddemann, "Agenda for a Gracious Revolution," *International Bulletin of Missionary Research* 23 (1999): 156-60.

[11]Ibid.

[12]Joseph D'Souza, "Telling It As It Is," *Evangelical Missions Quarterly*, October 1998, pp. 422-23.

[13]James F. Engel has written widely on the subject of donor marketing. See especially his first publication, *Averting the Financial Crisis in Christian Organizations: Insights from a Decade of Donor Research* (Orange, Calif.: Management Development Associates, 1983).

[14]See Engel, *Clouded Future?*

[15]Chuck Bennett, "Is There a Spin Doctor in the House?" *Evangelical Missions Quarterly*, October 1988, pp. 420-25.

[16]Engel, *Averting the Financial Crisis.*

[17]There is a large body of literature on this subject. See especially Michael Hammer and James Champy, *Reengineering the Corporation* (New York: Harper Business, 1993).

[18]See Phill Butler, *Partnership: Accelerating Evangelism in the 90s* (Seattle, Wash.: INTERDEV, n.d.).

[19]Kotter, "Winning at Change," p. 27.

Chapter 7: Missions in a Postmodern World: Will the Clouds Lift?

[1]See especially David J. Bosch, *Transforming Christian Mission* (Maryknoll, N.Y.: Orbis, 1991); Lesslie Newbigin, *The Gospel in a Pluralistic Society* (Grand Rapids, Mich.: Eerdmans, 1989); Mark Noll, *The Scandal of the Evangelical Mind* (Grand Rapids, Mich.: Eerdmans, 1994); and Os Guinness, *The Gravedigger File* (Downers Grove, Ill.: InterVarsity Press, 1983).

[2]See especially Bosch, *Transforming Christian Mission*, chaps. 10, 11. He stresses the three points that follow.

[3]We are borrowing once again Jim Plueddemann's phrasing here, because it aptly captures the spirit of a new millennium. See James Plueddemann, "SIM's Agenda for a Gracious Revolution," *International Bulletin of Missionary Research* 23 (1999): 156-60.